"Paul Farmer is one of the most extraordinary people I have ever met. A brilliant doctor and teacher, he tirelessly works for the poorest of the poor, insisting that they deserve the very best care that is available. He not only changes individual lives, but massive systems, proving against overwhelming objections that his methods are not only what Christian compassion demands, but that they bring about effective cures. Jennie Weiss Block will make you fall in love not only with Paul, but with the beloved people to whom he is so passionately committed. This is not a book you can put back on the shelf after reading; it will move you to take the next step in your own commitment to accompany the poorest in our world."

—Barbara Reid, OP
　　Professor of New Testament Studies
　　Catholic Theological Union

"It is rare that readers get to explore the lives of legendary people while they are still with us making this book a precious gift. One of the greatest physician-scholar-activist servants in American history, Paul Farmer is a powerful model of service to the poor. The world has much to learn from his life and witness. For anyone with a heart for the vulnerable, the poor, and the underserved, this thoughtful new text about an extraordinary human being is an inspiration and must-read."

—Bryan Stevenson
　　Director of Equal Justice Initiative and author of *Just Mercy*

"Some say that the devil is in the details, but in the life of Paul Farmer, there's grace in those details! Whether he's living in Haiti, Liberia, Rwanda, or Cambridge, channeling the corporal works into weapons of mass salvation, or running with the preferential option for the poor, Paul's life exudes the call that's so tangible in these pages. His friend and spiritual adviser, Jennie Weiss Block, captures it all in her compelling account when she asks us, 'How do you say no to someone who takes the Gospel so seriously?' Read this beautiful book and see if you too don't find yourself saying, 'Yes!'"

—James F. Keenan, SJ
　　Canisius Professor, Boston College

People of God

Remarkable Lives, Heroes of Faith

People of God is a series of inspiring biographies for the general reader. Each volume offers a compelling and honest narrative of the life of an important twentieth- or twenty-first-century Catholic. Some living and some now deceased, each of these women and men has known challenges and weaknesses familiar to most of us but responded to them in ways that call us to our own forms of heroism. Each offers a credible and concrete witness of faith, hope, and love to people of our own day.

More titles to follow . . .

Paul Farmer

Servant to the Poor

Jennie Weiss Block

LITURGICAL PRESS
Collegeville, Minnesota

www.litpress.org

Cover design by Red+Company. Cover illustration by Philip Bannister.

1	2	3	4	5	6	7	8	9

Library of Congress Control Number: 2018946265

ISBN 978-0-8146-4574-1   978-0-8146-4500-0 (e-book)

For my grandchildren
Sander, Annabelle, Jay and Daisy

Contents

Acknowledgments

If the only prayer you ever say in your entire life is
thank you, it will be enough.

Meister Eckhart

Anyone who has written a book knows two things. First,
while writing is a mostly solitary endeavor, the process of
bringing a book to fruition requires assistance from many
people. Second, writing a book requires a significant amount
of focus and energy, along with huge blocks of time apart.
This inevitably means that there will be times when the
writer will be unavailable, and this time apart can cause, at
the very least, some inconvenience or perhaps even some
hardship, especially to those who are closest to the writer.
Thus, with great gratitude, I would like to recognize the
many people who fall into these two categories—those who
assisted me in bringing this book to completion; and my
family, my religious community, and my friends—for their
support, understanding, and good humor during the many
months I worked on this book.

It has been a privilege to contribute to the People of God
series, and I am grateful to Liturgical Press for giving me

the opportunity to share the life and work of Paul Farmer with a new audience. To Barry Hudock, thank you for your patience and guidance throughout the project. Thanks to Christina Nichols for her expert editing advice, and to Stephanie Lancour for her assistance moving this book through the production phase.

I am deeply grateful to the many extraordinary colleagues and friends—too numerous to list individually—I have met through my work with Partners In Health, Harvard University, and the United Nations. Each of you is an inspiration, and I send my thanks, my love, and my admiration for your fortitude and untiring efforts to improve the lives of the world's poorest people. Special thanks to the fantastic people with whom I work most closely on a daily basis, especially Loune Viaud, Katie Kralievits, Abbey Gardner, Jehane Sedky, Gretchen Williams, Liz Campa, and Ishaan Desai. Please know how much I love working with you and how much I appreciate your support for this book project and your prompt and detailed responses to my many requests for source material and fact checking.

It is a joy to know all the members of the Farmer-Bertrand family, and I am grateful for all we have shared throughout the years. Paul's mother, Ginny Farmer, the matriarch of their family, is a role model for all of us. Special thanks to Jennifer and Jeff for their help answering questions and fact checking.

I owe a huge debt to Tracy Kidder for his beautiful book, *Mountains Beyond Mountains,* which has been an invaluable source of information and insight. Thank you to Jim Nickoloff for his excellent editing assistance and advice. This is a much better book because of his efforts, although I take full responsibility for any errors. I am grateful to my readers, Jessica Cousett, Scott O'Brien, OP, Mary Block, and

Cathy Mazza Berkowitz for their feedback and suggestions. Thank you to Fr. Joe Driscoll for sharing his reflections on Fr. Jack and Paul's time at St. Mary of the Angels.

My assistant, Lisa Manoogian, has been by my side for over twenty-five years, and her handling many personal and business matters allowed me time to write. Her calm and competence are a great gift that I do not take for granted. Many thanks to Argentina Rivas, Ezelda Cornejo Miles, and Mellisa Banh for assistance with household matters.

I am blessed with a large extended family, devoted, lifelong friends, and a wonderful religious community, all of whom generously supported me in a variety of ways while I worked on this book. I am grateful for their unconditional love, good humor, and especially for never complaining about the times that I was unavailable while finishing this book.

To my Dominican brothers in the Province of St. Martin de Porres: Thank you for giving me a place in the church and the opportunity to preach the Gospel. I hope you see this book as part of our preaching ministry. Special thanks to my provincial, Tom Condon, OP, for his unfailing kindness and support. To Scott O'Brien, OP, Jorge Presmanes, OP, and Mark Wedig, OP, you have my enduring gratitude for your accompaniment and friendship for over two decades.

To the members of the "Family Weiss": Thanks to each of you for our solidarity and the deep sense of family that is the foundation of our lives. My sisters, Laurie Weiss Nuell and Lynn Booth Monnin, are a constant daily support and enrich my life in every respect. To our grown children and their spouses, Chris and Catherine, Mary and Sean, Genevieve and Zisko, Lizzi and Ryan, Robert and Tommy, and Molly; and to my great-nieces, Charley and Sophie, and my grandchildren, Sander, Annabelle, Jay, and Daisy: thank you for surrounding me with peace and light and revealing the mystery of God's love each and every day. I hope you will someday understand that our work on behalf of poor and marginalized people is done in large measure because we want you to inherit a world where stories of poverty and oppression are found only in history books.

And, finally to Paul Farmer: Thank you for making me believe that it is possible to build the kingdom of God on earth.

Jennie Weiss Block, OP
Miami, Florida
May 25, 2018
Feast of St. Madeline Sophie

Introduction

Whenever you enter a town and its people welcome
you, . . . cure the sick who are there, and say to
them, "The kingdom of God has come near to you."
Luke 10:8-9

The idea that some lives matter less is the root of
all that is wrong with the world.[1]
Paul Farmer

Once in a great while, you meet someone who makes you
believe that it is possible to build up the kingdom of God in
the here and now. For me and many others, Dr. Paul Farmer
is such a person. A simple story well illustrates my point.

Ten years ago, I spent several days in rural Haiti observing
Paul build a garden in the center of a hospital complex in
Lascahobas, only about forty-eight miles from Port-au-Prince
but a two-to-four-hour drive depending on the weather and
road conditions. The La Colline hospital, owed by the Haitian
government, built and operated by Partners In Health (PIH),
is reached by traveling down a partially paved road over
mostly rugged terrain made worse during the rainy season
by the thick mud. After bumping down the entrance road,

you come upon the long, one-story white hospital building set back on the left. It is a big hospital with an ambulatory care clinic, multiple examining and treatment rooms, and a pharmacy. Adjacent to the main building are several other smaller buildings, including an x-ray lab, a dental clinic, and a big kitchen where meals are prepared for the patients and no doubt many people from the surrounding neighborhood.

Entering the hospital under a wide covered porch, you pass through a set of attractively designed and locally made black wrought-iron gates. A large foyer leads to a center courtyard that, during my visit, was being transformed before my eyes into a beautiful garden for the patients and families at the hospital. On the far end of the garden was a large, three-sided wrought-iron bench that would soon be covered with thick vines for shade. Paul Farmer believes that trees and flowers and fishponds are an important and necessary part of the hospitals he helps build to serve the poorest people in the world. "Hospitals for the rich have beautiful gardens and landscaping . . . Why shouldn't hospitals for the poor?" he explained. Paul himself had drawn detailed plans for the garden on a large piece of white paper. He stopped frequently to unroll the paper and discuss the plan with his Haitian coworkers, two of whom had been trained in agriculture. Sitting in the area opposite the bench was the *pièce de résistance* of the garden—a huge, and I do mean huge, rock. As the already-growing legend has it, Paul spotted this rock, at least five feet in diameter, on the roadside miles from the hospital. Some seventy men were paid to move the rock to the hospital, where it now sat inside the garden wall on the edge of what would soon be a fishpond.

Over several days, Paul and his coworkers transformed the bare, dirt-floored courtyard into a lovely garden. The plants, trees, soil, and gravel all needed to be brought in over the rough roads from Port-au-Prince. Working conditions in Haiti are difficult; neither promised goods nor promised delivery times are assured. But the patient garden builders were not to be deterred, and slowly but surely the garden took shape. Flowers were planted, and heavy white stones, edged with monkey grass, were laid to form a path to the sitting area, which was then filled with gray gravel. Bushy bamboo trees appeared in the corners behind the giant rock. Asparagus ferns and bromeliads were nestled in the crevices of the rock. Thick bushes with red ginger blossoms filled in the area behind the rock, surrounded by bushes with little blue flowers. Spindly-armed plants were formed into a little bog, and a bright green, flowering ground cover was laid. Workers planted night-blooming jasmine in back of the benches so the patients could enjoy their sweet scent. A pump hidden under the greenery attached to a hose that ran through a piece of bamboo made a waterfall into the pond.

Dr. Farmer and his coworkers truly believe that nothing is too good or too much trouble for the poor. The extraordinary thing is that Paul and his colleagues at Partners In Health, the nonprofit he cofounded thirty years ago, care for eight *million* patients a year in Haiti and eleven other countries around the world with the same love, skill, and commitment I saw being poured into the building of this garden.

The raising of the garden was a major community happening. Every day, more and more Haitians from the local area gathered around the low wall to watch as their garden took shape. The ways in which this hospital and this garden change the lives of the community cannot be underestimated. The "dignity of every human person" is not just an ideological phrase but a tangible reality for Paul Farmer. All who enter through the iron gates receive medical care, free of charge, on par with the medical care provided in the hospitals affiliated with Harvard University, where Paul is a professor of medicine. No one who comes to this hospital languishes and dies from a treatable medical condition. Those who would have been doomed to certain death from malaria, tuberculosis, or HIV/AIDS instead receive state-of-the art treatment and medications. Routine medical care that the rich take for granted is available, and babies, even premature ones, are delivered safely. Jobs are created, the local community is empowered, drinkable water flows, and the deepest of human hungers is assuaged with both food and compassion.

The sense of joy during these garden-building days was palpable. The Haitian minister of health stopped by to see the progress, and a meal of rice, beans, and plantains appeared which seemed to multiply, New Testament–like, to feed the crowd. Ever thoughtful, Paul stopped his work to help me plant a tree in front of the hospital in memory of my husband Sandy, to mark the sixteenth anniversary of his death.

Late one afternoon as twilight drew near, Paul hopped up on the huge rock to survey the progress. As he stood there, in wrinkled clothes and a baseball cap, hands dirty from planting in the thick black soil, the crowd broke out into spontaneous applause and cheering. When he grinned and gave the thumbs up sign, I looked at Paul, and the newly planted flowers and trees, and the smiling faces of my Haitian brothers and sisters, and was overwhelmed with joy because I knew I was standing on holy ground and the kingdom of God was at hand. Yes, the kingdom of God in the here and now, being built upon a big rock where a community of hope will gather under a green canopy, in a garden filled with the scent of jasmine and the sound of a trickling waterfall.

Who is Paul Farmer? And what is it about him that makes one believe that it is indeed possible to build up the kingdom on earth? By any standard, his credentials and accomplishments are outstanding. Educated at Duke and Harvard, Dr. Paul Farmer is the Kolokotrones University Professor at Harvard University. He is a professor of medicine, and the chair of its Department of Global Health and Social Medicine at Harvard Medical School, and the chief of the Division of Global Health Equity at Brigham and Women's Hospital in Boston. Cofounder of the noted nonprofit organization Partners In Health, Dr. Farmer also serves as a special adviser to the secretary-general of the United Nations. The list of honors and awards Dr. Farmer has received goes on for pages in his ninety-five-page curriculum vitae. His intellectual gifts are extraordinary, but he is able to articulate complex ideas in an accessible way. He has authored hundreds of scholarly articles and authored or coauthored fifteen books. Tracy Kidder's best-selling book *Mountains Beyond Mountains: The Quest of Dr. Paul Farmer, a Man Who Would Cure the World* (which has sold over 1.5 million copies and has been translated into 9 languages) introduced Paul Farmer and the work of PIH to a worldwide audience. Most recently, his work has been featured in the award-winning documentary *Bending the Arc*. Sometimes referred to as a "nonprofit celebrity," Dr. Farmer is a hero and inspiration to many and often draws crowds in the thousands when speaking on college campuses.

All kinds of people are attracted to Paul, sensing in him something that is "not of this world." Although he is often called a saint, he would surely not refer to himself in this way—and I do not wish to paint an overly romantic picture of him. Like all people, including holy ones, he is complex and not without faults and idiosyncrasies, which he himself is often quick to point out. To his credit, he does not shy away from being "human," nor does he cling to any suggestion of perfection. A charismatic leader, Paul Farmer is charming and fun to be around—he has a great sense of humor—and is able to motivate and challenge people to be their best selves. He is kind and generous, always giving people the benefit of the doubt or making excuses for behavior that others find off-putting or unacceptable. He doesn't just give people a second chance, but sometimes a third or fourth, often annoying his colleagues. Sensitive and humble, he possesses an ability to observe keenly and listen intuitively that allows him to connect with people at a deep level. Determined and passionate, he can be demanding and exacting. Like many people who labor in the global health world, he struggles to find a work-life balance and time with his family, given his demanding travel schedule and the urgency of providing medical care for people whose lives depend on it. His decisions and actions are shaped by the moral demands of the Gospel of Jesus, which he takes with the utmost seriousness. His life's work among the destitute poor is a tangible sign of God's love and mercy and reveals him to be a person who believes in and experiences transcendence.

Writing this book presented me with three challenges. First, in a spirit of full disclosure, let me mention that I have had a close personal and professional relationship with Paul for over a decade, with all the privileges and biases this implies. My relationship with Paul Farmer began in April of 2005, when, of all things, I gave him some used furniture. I was introduced to Paul by our mutual friends, Lanny and Behna Gardner, whose daughter Abbey had worked with Paul in Russia in the late nineties. Lanny is a Harvard-trained doctor and at the time was the chief of medicine at the University of Miami. Behna is a professional photographer. Friends close to Paul and his wife, Didi Bertrand, were concerned about their financial future and suggested that owning a home would be a good decision both financially and personally. Paul and Didi decided they wanted to live in Miami, only a short flight from Haiti, where they both worked, and they asked Behna to help them with the process of finding and purchasing a house. Behna found the house online and showed it to Didi and Paul, and they liked it. The house was the first, and only, financial investment Paul has ever made. He was in the habit (and still is) of giving all his money away to the poor even faster than he earns it. Situated on a nice piece of property, the house was modest but comfortable for the family. Paul loved the many trees and the dense tropical landscaping and envisioned a garden and a fishpond. His first and only purchase for the new house was a big tree fern.

Behna had told me something about her wonderful doctor friend who was dedicated to the poor, and my sister had read *Mountains Beyond Mountains* and thought Paul and his work were fantastic. I didn't have time to read the book, as I was busy doing research in preparation for writing my doctoral thesis while also getting ready to move, downsizing to a much smaller home as my last child left for college. Grateful for Paul's work with the poor, I thought to ask Behna if the Farmer family were in need of any furniture. Since Paul's only purchase had been a plant, and the house was empty save for a mattress on the floor, Behna, on behalf of Paul, accepted my offer. Truth be told, while I was pleased to give some furniture to a doctor who served the poor, I wasn't particularly interested in meeting him. I thought he might be the type that "believed his own PR," if you know what I mean. One afternoon, several months after I delivered the furniture, Paul's mother, Ginny, called to invite me over to dinner so they could thank me for the furniture. Not wanting to be rude, I stopped by for what I thought would be a brief visit.

Along with Paul and Ginny, Paul's sister Katy and her husband Bob were there too, and they all greeted me warmly. Paul was sitting in a chair in the living room reading when I arrived. As he put his book down to stand up to greet me, I glanced down and saw the title of the book he was reading: *Selected Writings* by Meister Eckhart. Eckhart (1260–1328) was a German Dominican friar, brilliant theologian, and mystic. Erudite, profound, and dense, Meister Eckhart is not an easy read and definitely *not* what someone who believes his own PR would be reading. I couldn't help but ask, "You are reading Meister Eckhart?" "Trying to, but it is not easy," was Paul's humble reply. All these years later, we both still thank Meister Eckert for bringing us together.

Over the following years, I developed a great friendship with Paul and Didi and the Farmer and Bertrand families. My friendship with Paul is grounded in the spiritual life, and he often refers to me as his spiritual adviser (his "interior decorator," as he likes to joke). Our relationship has a pragmatic side—I soon became involved in supporting the work of Partners In Health. Four years later, in 2009, with much trepidation—I suppose because he knew the demands it would place on me—Paul asked me to come and work with him. The job was supposed to be a short-term assignment, but nine years later, I am still working as his chief adviser with responsibility for a wide range of policy and administrative functions. The kind of work we do is not really a job; I think of it more as a lifestyle, as it permeates all aspects of one's life. Now all the members of my family, even my young grandchildren, are involved in our work in one way or another.

Since 2009, I have traveled extensively with Paul throughout the developing world and have had the opportunity to observe him in many different contexts. Some of the stories and experiences shared in this book are ones I have observed firsthand. Of course, sensitivity is always required when exploring or revealing another's interior life, especially when the subject is still living. While Paul has given his blessing to this writing project (albeit hesitantly and with some embarrassment) and we agreed that he would not read the book prior to publication, I am aware that I have had access to Paul's innermost thoughts and feelings and have knowledge of personal situations that only a close friend would or should be privy to. I have thus taken care to respect certain boundaries while not compromising the honesty and openness a book of this type requires.

Second, while it is widely known that Paul's work has been influenced by theological thought, especially liberation theology, and the story of Paul's life and work has been well told both in *Mountains Beyond Mountains* and more recently in *Bending the Arc*, the ways in which Paul's faith and interior life shape who he is have not been publicly or openly explored in any explicit way. Those close to him are aware of his vivid religious imagination, his love of the liturgy, the Eucharist, and religious iconography, and his frequent use of religious language and religious symbolism in his daily life. And while Tracy Kidder points out that the way Paul interprets meaning is often "fundamentally religious,"[2] Paul rarely speaks of his personal faith in public settings; as Fr. Gustavo Gutiérrez, OP, aptly puts it, "Dr. Farmer is a bit shy and reluctant to expound on theology and spirituality."[3] Nevertheless, his embrace of a radical Christianity organized around a "preferential option for the poor" affects every dimension of his life. I approach sharing this aspect of Paul's life with a keen sense of responsibility and with the hope that I can do justice to describing the lived experience of his Christian faith, the depth of his spiritual life, and the ways in which the paschal mystery, especially the suffering of the Crucified One, informs his thoughts and actions.

My third challenge, and perhaps the most difficult, was my struggle to determine just what the purpose and focus of this book should be. Paul's peripatetic life and significant accomplishments in the field of global health are well documented (far better than I could ever hope to do) in Tracy Kidder's wonderful book *Mountains Beyond Mountains* (if you have not read it, you should) and in the beautiful documentary film *Bending the Arc*, released in 2017 (if you have not seen it, you should). His academic accomplishments have been recognized with Harvard's highest designation of university professor, and his large corpus of writings—much of it quite scholarly—has a dedicated audience. While these aspects of his life and his attractive persona make for a highly engaging narrative, I believe that each of these perspectives ultimately falls short and doesn't adequately describe the Paul Farmer who somehow makes others believe that it is possible to build the kingdom of God in the here and now. Thus, my goal in this book is to tell the Paul Farmer story from a different perspective, one that uses the interpretive lenses of theology and spirituality to describe a humble man who takes the Gospel to heart, loves his neighbor as himself, and freely and unstintingly puts his life and his gifts at the service of the human community, especially the poor and marginalized among us.

To write a book that accomplishes this ambitious goal, especially within the length required by the publisher, it has been necessary to narrow its scope and carefully select what to include from a vast amount of information and source material. This inevitably means leaving out many significant events in Paul's life as well as important stories related to

Paul's and PIH's work in many countries around the globe.[4] It especially pains me to leave out important people and relationships in Paul's life, and I beg the forgiveness of those who are not included in these pages and hope they understand that it is only because of the limitations of space.

This book follows a loose chronological time line and makes extensive use of narrative stories, Dr. Farmer's own words taken from his writing and speeches, and the impressions and comments of others. The following overarching concepts helped to narrow my focus and guided my selection of material:

1. Paul's lifelong and total commitment to making a preferential option for the poor in health care, which has taken many forms over the last thirty years.

2. Paul's unusual but highly successful career as both a respected scholar and an effective implementer, which has forged a new model that links theory and praxis—in a hermeneutical circle of research, teaching, advocacy, and service—to advance his global health equity agenda.

3. The role that partnerships and deep and lasting friendships play in Paul's life. In particular, I have paid specific attention to the many significant relationships Paul has forged with the priests, nuns, theologians, and laypeople who have modeled the Christian life for him, nurtured his faith, and supported his work.

Finally, it is my hope that this book will be more than just an engaging story about a great doctor who has dedicated his life to serving the poor; I hope it will stir in the reader some desire to make common cause with those who suffer from the scandal of poverty. If this were not my aim, I am sure Paul would have preferred that this book not be written.

CHAPTER ONE

A Bus, a Boat, and Some Big Ideas

And the Word became flesh and lived among us, and we have seen his glory, the glory as of a father's only son, full of grace and truth.

John 1:14

My father was not a very orthodox guy. We actually lived in a tuberculosis bus for ten years. Back in the 60's, the public health service did TB screenings with mobile X-ray units. Then they sold them in public auctions, and my father, then a schoolteacher, bought one and moved in his eight family members. . . . This makes my biography sound a little too neat. I mean we grew up in a TB bus and I became a TB doctor. We worked picking citrus for about a nanosecond before my father admitted we could never make enough for us to live on, and years later I would [do the same] with Haitian migrant farmworkers. But it can be too neat and still be true, right?[1]

Paul Farmer

A God Dwelling Among Us

Paul and I were once talking about the incarnation. I was remarking about the utter mystery of a God who became human and "pitched his tent among us" when Paul grabbed a map of Haiti that was sitting on his coffee table, pointed to it, and said with great intensity, "I will show you how God is made flesh and living among us." He took a black Sharpie pen and drew the long route over which a desperately ill young boy was carried to the new, state-of-the-art teaching hospital that Partners In Health had just built in Mirebalais on Haiti's Central Plateau. A community health worker carried the boy on his back many hours over rough terrain from Léogâne to Mirebalais. Paul had been consulting on the case all day by phone with clinicians at the hospital, so the plight of this boy was on his mind. For Paul, God had again broken into human history through a sick child representing the spirit of Jesus in the flesh, crying out for help, through a Haitian peasant who loved his neighbor so much that he was willing to carry a sick child on his back for hours to save his life, and through the medical staff who stood ready to see Jesus' own face in the suffering child and give their all to save his life.

Paul grew up with two devout Catholic grandmothers; perhaps they planted the seeds of what would become his intense religious imagination. Second in a family of six children—three boys and three girls—Paul Edward Farmer Jr. was born on October 26, 1959, in North Adams, Massachusetts. His mother, Virginia Rice, dropped out of college to marry Paul Farmer Sr. when she was twenty years old, and had six babies in the following eight-year span. Years later, when the children were raised, she would return to Smith College and earn a degree in library science. In 1966, when Paul was nine years old, the family moved south to Birmingham, Alabama, for Paul Sr. to pursue a job in sales. PJ, as his family called him, and his siblings attended church as children, and their parents dutifully made sure they received the sacraments of initiation, but religion did not play a big part in their family life. By the time they were teenagers, church attendance had fallen by the wayside, and for Paul, the Catholic Church seemed perfunctory. As he recalls, "To me and my siblings, church was a place one went to fulfill obligations to parents and grandparents: First Communion, Confirmation, high holy days. It meant sitting through homilies—often boring ones, I'm sorry to say, and almost always remote from our experience. Perhaps the priests made too little effort or felt little need to make the effort to address people our age; more likely, we made too little effort ourselves."[2]

A Bus and a Boat to Call Home

Paul's father, Paul Sr., was what one might refer to as a "character." A large man in both size and personality, he was, in his own way, devoted to his family, although the lifestyle he fashioned for them was anything but traditional. In Birmingham, the family lived in a modest house, but in 1971, Paul Sr. packed up the family again and moved to Brooksville, Florida, where the family took up residence in a big bus, a former tuberculosis mobile clinic, which the family christened with the cheerful name of The Blue Bird Inn. Paul Sr. drove the bus to a trailer park at the Brentwood Lake Campground, where the family would live for five years. The bus was fitted with bunk beds for the children, a small curtained-off area for the parents, and a kitchen table. They kept their belongings in boxes under the bunk beds, and the entire family used the bathhouse at the campground. Paul's sisters have told me how difficult it was for them to live on the bus with little or no privacy or creature comforts, but the boys didn't seem to mind it as much and probably enjoyed exploring the nearby woods.

Paul's father got a job teaching math and English at the local public high school, which all of his children attended, and his mother, Ginny, worked as a cashier at a Winn-Dixie grocery store. Their family life didn't exactly fit the profile of what one might expect from their humble living conditions in a trailer park. There were high expectations for the children at school and at home; there was order and discipline, so much so that the girls nicknamed their strict father "the Warden." Reading was encouraged at home, the children were taken to the library to check out books, and the parents often read aloud in the evenings from Shakespeare and the classics. Despite the crowded quarters and the many practical inconveniences such as the lack of a bathroom or running water (which meant they had to use public bathroom facilities and fill empty milk jugs with water from an outdoor faucet at the local grocery store to carry home for drinking water), the Farmer family life was stable, and the children received lots of attention from both parents—unconditional love and support from their calm mother and active involvement in all aspects of their lives from their father. All in all, it was certainly a very unusual childhood, but in a *New York Times* interview Paul reflected, "When we were growing up in the campground, we were all sort of embarrassed by it, but I think all of us feel grateful to my parents for having liberated us from middle-class expectations."[3] And truth be told, none of the six Farmer children, all of whom have gone on to live productive and successful personal and professional lives, seem any worse for the wear.

Paul's intellectual gifts were apparent early, and he was placed in the "gifted" program in elementary school. By the fourth grade, he had become an avid reader, a habit that continues to this day. His favorite book was *The Lord of the Rings*. No doubt its religious imagery and symbolism appealed to his developing religious imagination, as did *War and Peace*, which he read for the first time when he was eleven years old.

About the same time Paul started at Hernando High School in Brooksville, his father moved the family to a boat that was moored at Jenkins Creek, a bayou on the Gulf Coast. Paul Sr. bought the boat at a public auction and named it *Lady Gin*, after his wife. It was an old Liberty Launch, about fifty feet long with holes that he repaired himself. He built a cabin with beds and a small living space, put in a generator, and hatched a plan that included using the boat both as the family home and as an income-producing commercial fishing boat. After several failed attempts at navigation out on the open waters, including a few incidents in stormy weather that scared Ginny Farmer, the boat was docked near land and the commercial fishing idea abandoned. There was a plank board to cross from dry land to the boat. Sometimes people ask why Ginny always went along with her husband's schemes, but as she told Tracy Kidder, "You didn't argue with Paul, Sr., you just didn't."[4] Paul would live on the boat with his family until he left for college. By all accounts, life on the bayou was not easy. They did not have running water, and the boat leaked when it rained; there was only a small fridge that had to be restocked constantly. His mother hated the bugs and roaches, and there were alligators in the swamp water. Paul didn't mind though, as he had—and still has—an affinity for reptiles and amphibians. He was happy too, that on a patch of land near the boat, he was able to plant his first garden and build his first fishpond, financing the costs with money he earned at a part-time job as a bag boy at a local grocery store.

Paul's relationship with his father was not always easy. There was an expectation that the boys would excel in competitive sports. His two younger brothers, Jim and Jeff, were big guys, built like their father. Paul, of much slighter build, tried very hard to participate in the school sports programs as was expected. But he ended up falling short in this area, a source of embarrassment and disappointment during his teen years. His father, who clearly fiercely loved his children, was on the gruff side and tended to withhold approval, even though he was quietly proud of Paul's academic achievements and would often brag to others about him—but only when Paul was out of earshot. Perhaps some of Paul's deep compassion for others was learned from his father, who taught at an alternative school for "at-risk" youth in the last years of his life. He was also very involved as a volunteer at an organization that served people with disabilities, probably because of his experience with his younger brother, Paul's uncle James. Several of Paul's siblings have shared stories with me about their Uncle Jim. Jennifer Farmer, one of Paul's younger sisters, explained the relationship:

> Dad was the oldest of six. His younger brother (directly after him in the birth order), contracted German measles and suffered swelling of the brain, causing severe and permanent mental damage. Uncle Jim, as we all knew him, was stuck in a state hospital in Massachusetts because that's what parents did in that day. Dad was never comfortable with that. As soon as his father (Grampa Farmer) died, Dad flew to Massachusetts and pulled him out of the institution and moved him to a group home near us in Brooksville. Dad picked him up at the group home nearly

every weekend and brought him home to stay with us on the weekends. Uncle Jim LOVED Dad and followed him around everywhere. When Dad died, Jim kept walking around trying to find him. It was terrible. He never understood where his big brother went.[5]

Paul Sr. insisted that Uncle Jim be welcomed into the family. Jim needed a great deal of support with daily activities, including dressing, bathing, toileting, and feeding, and his speech and communication skills were limited. Jennifer told me that her father always treated his brother with patience and compassion and expected the same from his children. As Jennifer puts it, "I know Dad was the first person that ever made Jim feel like he had a real family. I am sure this deeply impressed all of us. It's not that Dad ever said anything or preached about how we should take care of others who can't take care of themselves. It's just that he did it because he really loved his brother and he couldn't bear the thought of him being alone."[6]

Paul excelled in high school; his grades were excellent, and he was president of his senior class and very popular, especially with the girls. All of the Farmer children liked to participate in after-school activities and clubs, partly to avoid coming home to the cramped living quarters and the many chores their father had lined up for them.

In 2008, Paul returned to Brooksville to accept the honor of being named "Great Brooksvillian of the Year." Julia Jenkins, who nominated him, said she didn't think that he would come. "I thought maybe his mom would come and accept for him," Jenkins said of the award. "Instead, he not only accepted in person, but he was accompanied by his mother, Ginny, his daughter, Catherine, one of his sisters, and both brothers. Here he is, trotting around the globe, saving lives, and he makes time to come back to sleepy old Brooksville."[7] There was a weekend of festivities, including a party organized by his high-school friends, many of whom he has kept in close contact with throughout the years, a ride in the city's annual Christmas parade, and the Great Brooksvillian presentation at city hall, followed by a fund-raiser that netted about fifty thousand dollars for Partners In Health. Paul enjoyed every minute of it.

On Saturday afternoon, there was a book-signing event in the library. The line snaked around the building, and many of his high-school teachers came to see their former student. He greeted each and every person from his high-school years, remembering everyone's name. He did not rush anyone, stopping again and again for a picture or to recall a story about his relationship with the person, including thanking the registrar for giving him a pass to get into class without penalty when he was late to school.

One of the people who came to the book signing was his high-school guidance counselor, Wendy Tellone, to whom Paul owes a great debt of gratitude, for she was one who sensed in a young Paul Farmer much potential. She helped him apply to Duke University, where he was given a full scholarship. Paul jumped up to hug her, and she was just beaming. Needless to say, she let everyone know she was not at all surprised by his intellectual achievements and professional success.

Duke: The Birthplace of Some Big Ideas

Paul arrived at Duke in the fall of 1978. He was eighteen years old, excited to be away from home and out from under his father's strict watch. He was unsophisticated and curious, ready to take on the big world beyond rural Central

Florida. Given his unconventional childhood living conditions, a bedroom with his own closet, indoor plumbing, and hot showers were new experiences. He immediately took advantage of the wide variety of cultural and social opportunities offered and went, for the first time in his life, to the theatre and art galleries. He joined a fraternity, where he learned to party, even becoming the social director; however, he ended up resigning because he didn't want to belong to an all-white organization. One of his fraternity brothers was John Dear, who would become a Jesuit priest and an internationally known peace activist.

Paul was initially taken with the affluence he encountered in many of his Duke classmates, impressed by the trappings of wealth some of his friends enjoyed. However, in time as he got his bearings, he realized that the perks of wealth didn't really hold his interest or attention. He was much more interested in ideas, relationships, and service to others. He instinctively knew that accumulating wealth would not ever satisfy his deepest longings, and as he matured, he came to understand that he was much better suited for a life of service.

Paul's genuine interest in other people and total lack of pretentiousness, which he still maintains, made him very popular among his peers. Among the many friendships he formed at Duke was with Todd McCormack, who would become one of the cofounders of Partners In Health and is among Paul's closest friends to this day. Godfather to several of Anne and Todd McCormack's children, Paul has his own room in the McCormack home in Newton, Massachusetts, where he stays when in Boston. Todd just smiles and shakes his head when he finds Paul in his closet borrowing his socks and shirts just as he did during their college days. These days, Paul is on friendly terms with many billionaires who generously support his work at Harvard and Partners In Health, and while he is very grateful for their friendship, he still has no interest in accumulating wealth, nor does he put any effort into building his financial future. Many of his wealthy friends find this both admirable and a little disconcerting.

Paul spent some months in Paris during his junior year. He explored the city, soaked in French culture and history, and discovered his facility for languages, picking up French quickly. He studied with the famed anthropologist Claude Lévi-Strauss at the École des Hautes Études en Sciences Sociales, and his first international experience continued to broaden his worldview.

Paul's four years at Duke were profoundly formative and set the course for the rest of his life, especially in two significant ways: first, through his intellectual growth; and second, through a series of adult conversion experiences. He was a perfect candidate for the rigorous academic coursework offered at Duke and ripe for mentoring by faculty who no doubt saw extraordinary promise in him. He met progressive activists who awakened him to social and economic issues and challenged his thinking and worldview. Reading voraciously, he encountered the thinking of great minds by studying a wide range of disciplines, including social medicine, pathology, anthropology, sociology, political science, and history. He read books that, as he so aptly puts it, "cracked my mind open."[8] He started out as a biochemistry major but changed his major to medical anthropology in his junior year because his coursework in anthropology "just opened a whole new world."[9]

Paul was particularly influenced by the work of Rudolf Virchow (1821–1902), a brilliant and accomplished German physician who is often referred to as the founder of social medicine. Along with his medical practice, Virchow was also an anthropologist, a pathologist, a biologist, a writer, and an editor, and he is recognized for advancing the fields of pathology and public health. While Virchow's scholarly writings no doubt made an impression on Paul, it was Virchow's synthetic model of integrating multiple disciplines and linking scholarship with implementation that captured his imagination. Paul would go on to emulate Virchow in his own work, forging a discipline that integrates medicine and anthropology with praxis.

A Faith Worth Dying For

There comes a time for many, perhaps most, Catholics when they must leave behind the faith of their childhood— no matter how good or bad the religious formation was— and decide whether they will embrace the faith in their adult lives. Some decide to move on, leaving the church and the faith behind. Others, often because of an adult conversion experience, see the Christian faith in a new way and make it their own. While at Duke, Paul had a series of adult conversion experiences that revealed to him a dimension of the faith that changed his ideas about the Catholic faith and the church. A seminal event occurred on March 24, 1980, the terrible day Archbishop Óscar Romero was gunned down while celebrating Mass in a hospital chapel in San Salvador, El Salvador. Paul describes it this way: "I stood in front of the Duke Chapel with more than a hundred fellow mourners, gathered in shock to grieve for the murder of Romero. He had been cut down in the middle of Mass while intoning the very words, no doubt, that had recently seemed to me so dull and uninspiring."[10] He once told me that during the candlelight vigil, as he contemplated Romero's life and death, he internalized the idea that there was a radical edge to Christianity that some embrace even unto death; it is "a faith worth dying for," in Paul's own words. Or, as he told Tracy Kidder, "Wow! This ain't the Catholicism that I remember."[11]

The first of many significant relationships with religious people that Paul would develop over the years began at Duke when he met Sr. Julianna DeWolf, a "social justice nun," as he affectionately refers to her. She and a group of sisters from her congregation were working with the United Farm Workers on behalf of the migrant farm workers in the area, many of whom were Haitians. Paul volunteered with Sr. Julianna's group and saw firsthand the terrible conditions that migrant workers endured in their labor camps. Paul was impressed with the work ethic of the sisters; Sr. Julianna was hard-core, willing to do any job that was needed, no matter the cost, and fearless when standing up to injustice. As he told Tracy Kidder, "They were the ones standing up to the growers in their sensible nun shoes. They were the ones schlepping the workers to the clinics or courts, translating for them, getting them groceries or driver's licenses."[12]

When Sr. Julianna took the time to take Paul on tours of some of the migrant camps, he had another conversion of sorts, experiencing what Belgian Dominican theologian Edward Schillebeeckx calls a "negative contrast experience." Negative contrast experiences occur when we encounter a situation where human suffering is occurring and we know what we are seeing is terribly wrong, especially when we are forced to compare it with another, more positive experience with which we are familiar. This experience often creates a sense of moral outrage and drives people towards working for justice. In Paul's case, he saw his life at Duke—with its many comforts, unlimited opportunities, and access to the goods and services that make human flourishing possible—standing in stark contrast to the miserable lives of the migrant workers living just a few miles away with almost no opportunity. He was upset; it made him anxious because he knew he was seeing great injustice, although he did not yet understand the complex social and economic forces that create systematic injustice and oppression.

Talking to some Haitians he met in the migrant camps piqued Paul's interest in Haiti, and he began to read Haitian history and culture. It was around this time that Paul was also introduced to liberation theology and the notion of a preferential option for the poor. He began to read Gustavo Gutiérrez, Jon Sobrino, and other Latin American theologians who would come to have a significant influence on his thinking and his medical work. Liberation theology is a theological movement rooted in the social movements for freedom that arose in Latin America in the 1960s. Liberation theology seeks to interpret the Scriptures and the Christian tradition in light of efforts to overcome the scandal of poverty and oppression. Taking the view "from below"—that is, from the perspective of the poor—liberation theology attempts to identify the "structural sins" that create terrible poverty for billions of people in the world and contrasts this reality with the kingdom of God that Jesus preached. Liberation theology challenges individual Christians, the church as a whole, and even non-Christians to make a preferential option for the poor, to work towards eliminating unjust structures and conditions, and to build a more just world. While liberation theology has provoked a good bit of controversy, the church's magisterium has affirmed its useful and necessary role.

All in all, his years at Duke were an extraordinary time of intellectual, personal, and spiritual growth, and Paul remains deeply grateful to Duke, where he is a now a member of the board of trustees and a generous donor to the scholarship programs that offer others the life-changing opportunity he was afforded. Another Duke graduate, Melinda Gates, was the 2013 commencement speaker, and she had this to say about Paul:

> Paul Farmer, the Duke graduate I admire most, is a testament to the deep human connection that I am talking about. As many of you know, Paul, who is here today, is a doctor and a global health innovator. I first met Paul in 2004, when I went to see him in Haiti. It took us forever to walk the 100 yards from our vehicle to the clinic because he introduced me to every single person we met along the way. I am not exaggerating. Every single person.
>
> As we moved along, he introduced each person to me by first and last name, wished their families well, and asked for an update about their lives. He hugged people when he greeted them and looked them in the eyes through each conversation. If you believe love plays a role in healing, there was healing happening at every step of that journey.
>
> When we finally reached the waiting area outside the clinic, I saw a lovely garden with a canopy of flowering vines. Paul told me he built it himself, for two reasons. First, he said, it gets hot, and he wants his patients to be cool in the shade while they wait. Second, he wants them to see what he sees, the beauty of the world, before they have to go into the clinic for treatment.[13]

Paul graduated from Duke on a sunny day in May of 1982. Unlike many young people who have no idea what they want to be or do, Paul had a very clear idea of how he wanted to spend the rest of his life. He claims that he knew he wanted to be a doctor from the time he was quite young. "I always wanted to be a doctor, I say always. Why on earth? I don't know. In fact, I never really met any doctors when I was young. I never received any real medical care, except for when I broke my arm and that was like an hour in the emergency room. And that was it. So I must have been enchanted with the idea of being a physician. I certainly was set on it by the time I went off to college."[14] His ideas about how he was going to practice medicine developed at Duke and were influenced by his great mentor, Virchow, and his comprehensive vision of integrating medicine, anthropology, and praxis.

Paul notes that he chose anthropology, specifically medical anthropology, much more carefully, much more thoughtfully, than he made his youthful decision to become a doctor. Anthropology appealed to him because it was both a process that revealed meaning and a way to pay attention to and understand the complex realities of people's lives. It taught him to search "for how people are socialized, what worldviews, cosmologies, understandings, beliefs, praxis they bring to their everyday life."[15] His ideas about the kind of medicine he wanted to practice were informed by liberation theology, with its view of the world from the perspective of the poor, and the unmasking of the structural sin that creates the crushing poverty that billions of people endure. He had no doubt that making a preferential option for the poor with the goal of lessening human suffering would be his life's work. Although he would likely not put it in these terms, he was developing what I would call an "unconventional piety." By this, I mean a *rugged spirituality* (like that of Óscar Romero) that finds its meaning in a revolutionary, radical commitment; a *compassionate spirituality* (like that of the militant nuns in the migrant camps) that is rooted in Jesus' commandment to love your neighbor as yourself; and an *intense spirituality* (like that of Gustavo Gutiérrez) rooted in the willingness to encounter the face of the Crucified One in the faces of the suffering of the world's poor. Over time, as Paul embraced and internalized his religious experiences, his faith deepened into an *action-oriented spirituality* rooted in the deep desire to tend and mend the world's wounds by bringing the medicine of expert mercy to his suffering brothers and sisters.

In May of 2005, at a commencement address at Boston College, Paul would tell the graduates what had been clear to him on his own graduation day, twenty-three years earlier: "You will—you must—find out about the world's wounds. My own guess is that poverty and powerlessness and untreated disease are hell on earth and that there is nothing God-given about such conditions. They are 'man'-given. And if hell can be created by human beings rather than some inescapable force of God or nature, we humans might just have a salvific role to play."[16]

What was not exactly clear on that sunny day in May of 1982 when Paul graduated from Duke was where, how, and with whom he would make his lofty moral goals come to fruition. But he did not let the unknown dampen his motivation or enthusiasm as he set out into the world.

CHAPTER TWO

The Corporal Works of Mercy

Weapons of Mass Salvation

> Then the righteous will answer him, "Lord, when was it that we saw you hungry and gave you food, or thirsty and gave you something to drink? And when was it that we saw you a stranger and welcomed you, or naked and gave you clothing? And when was it that we saw you sick or in prison and visited you?" And the king will answer them, "Truly I tell you, just as you did it to one of the least of these who are members of my family, you did it to me."
>
> Matthew 25:37-40

> Partners In Health is a secular organization, but all of us embrace the corporal works of mercy laid out clearly enough in the Gospels (Matthew 25:34). These are not vague injunctions. Feed the hungry. Give drink to the thirsty. Clothe the naked. Shelter the homeless. Visit the sick. Visit prisoners. Bury the dead.[1]
>
> Paul Farmer

I read last week that the current US administration has spent $191 billion on wars in the Middle East. Imagine if we had even half of that war chest, the mere bagatelle of $95.5 billion, for weapons of mass

salvation. In contrast to certain Weapons of Mass
Destruction, these weapons do exist. They are vac-
cines and programs of prevention and care; they are
decent sanitation and enough to eat. And don't you
wonder if attacking the social problems of the bottom billion might be a more effective means of
expunging terrorism than some of the current strategies being employed?[2]

Paul Farmer

Fr. Gerry and the Blood Run

On Christmas Day in 2005, Paul called me from his
mother's house in Orlando to ask me for the exact wording
and citation from Matthew's gospel when Jesus is asked,
"Lord, when was it we saw you sick and in prison?" He
needed the citation for an article he was writing, entitled
"Christmas in a Haitian Jail," that was subsequently published in the *Miami Herald* on January 2, 2006, telling the
world of the plight of Fr. Gérard Jean-Juste, a seriously ill
political prisoner in Haiti. Fr. Gerry, as he was affectionately
called, was a Catholic priest, defender of the Haitian poor,
and revolutionary of sorts, often in trouble with the church
hierarchy for infractions such as conducting funeral services
for refugees who had drowned at sea, regardless of their
religious background. Sometimes referred to as the Martin
Luther King Jr. of Haiti, Fr. Gerry was someone Paul considered a good friend.

In mid-December, Paul had gotten word that Fr. Gerry's
health was deteriorating. He had swelling on both sides of
his neck that he initially thought was due to a beating he
had received in jail. But now the swelling was increasing,
he had swollen lymph nodes elsewhere, and he was very

fatigued. Paul was really worried. He decided that he must go to the prison during his trip to Haiti the following week; he hoped he could get into the prison, examine Fr. Gerry, and draw blood for testing. Paul was getting significant resistance to this plan from friends and colleagues who believed, with good cause, that even attempting to visit, let alone examining Fr. Gerry and drawing blood, was a terrible idea as well as a dangerous mission. But Paul was not to be deterred. On the morning of December 23, Paul left Cange at four o'clock in the morning for the long drive back to Port-au-Prince. He arrived at the prison around nine o'clock, planning to take the two o'clock flight back to Miami. He was not sure if the prison would let him see Fr. Gerry, but he managed to talk his way in and afterwards called me on his way to the airport. Fr. Gerry had insisted on some singing and praying and then allowed Paul to do a quick examination and to surreptitiously draw two vials of blood while other prisoners distracted the guards. Paul asked me, "Do you think you can find a doctor in Miami who can help with a diagnosis? I was only able to get two tubes of blood, and time is of the essence as the blood will not hold up for long." How do you say no to someone who takes the Gospel so seriously?

There were many obstacles. It was late in the afternoon two days before Christmas, not exactly the best time to be seeking immediate medical assistance. Paul was entering the United States with contraband blood belonging to a controversial political figure, and there were other sticky matters such as patient confidentiality and the problem of payment for a series of very expensive tests. A brilliant University of Miami hematologist and an old family friend, Dr. Y. S. Ahn, was pressed into service and agreed to help. As soon as Paul landed, he went straight to the hospital, where

Dr. Ahn was waiting outside for him. It was growing dark, and things were shutting down for the holiday, but Dr. Ahn promised to run the tests himself and get back to us as soon as possible. Two hours later, Dr. Ahn called and gave Paul a diagnosis: acute chronic lymphocytic leukemia. Both doctors knew that with proper treatment, Fr. Gerry had a good prognosis. However, because this type of cancer can quickly develop into a more aggressive type, Fr. Gerry needed immediate treatment.

Paul called the prison, and given the news he was reporting, he was allowed to speak to Fr. Gerry. He told him of his diagnosis and the plans to bring him to Miami for treatment, although exactly how Paul was going to get him out of prison and to Miami was unclear. Various human rights groups, including Amnesty International, and forty-two members of the US House of Representatives, led by Maxine Waters, had been calling for Fr. Gerry's release from prison for months to no avail, but the report of his deteriorating health gave the situation added urgency.

Paul was certain that the only person who could assist with Fr. Gerry's release was Secretary of State Condoleezza Rice, so we turned to another family friend, Republican Congresswoman Ileana Ros-Lehtinen. She surely knew of Fr. Gerry's situation, as it had been receiving widespread publicity, so at Paul's urging, I gathered my courage and sent her an e-mail asking if she would be willing to help. She was on a ski vacation with her family and responded quickly on her Blackberry with the following message. "I am not a big fan of his but if he is your friend, I guess he is my new best pal." One never quite knows what goes on behind the scenes in political matters, but a week later Paul's colleague Harvard doctor Jennifer Furin was on her way to Haiti to escort Fr. Gerry to the States for medical treatment at Jackson Memorial Hospital in Miami. His treatment was rigorous and exhausting but successful, and eight months later, his doctors pronounced him in remission.[3]

Growing in Grace, Courage, and Compassion

How does one become the kind of person who takes the corporal works of mercy so seriously that he is willing to go into a Haitian prison to draw blood from a critically ill prisoner knowing full well that this act could have disastrous personal consequences? What kind of formation makes a person bold enough to write an editorial in a major newspaper calling out injustice without regard for possible damage to one's own standing and reputation? And willing to ask one's friends to help no matter the imposition or cost? What is the wellspring of this kind of courage and compassion?

The qualities of courage and compassion, so evident in the mature Paul Farmer, were not yet fully formed when Paul graduated from college, but rather took shape and emerged in a slow awakening. Disparate events, both positive and negative, along with what can only be called grace-filled experiences and relationships, would form him morally and educate him in virtue. After graduating from Duke in May of 1982, Paul took what is now referred to as a "gap" year. He had hoped to head to Africa to pursue some ethnographic work. He often tells students today not to give up when things don't go their way; he shares how he applied for a Fulbright Scholarship to go study and work in Africa and didn't even get an interview, so he ended up going to Haiti instead. The students all love this story; it is along the same lines as Michael Jordan being cut from his college basketball team.

When Africa didn't pan out, Paul decided to spend his gap year in Haiti, while he was applying to medical school.

He had become interested in Haitian history and culture at Duke and planned to try to view the country using his anthropological and ethnographic training as well as volunteer in a medical setting as he prepared to attend medical school. Before his trip to Haiti, he had completed a short postgraduate fellowship at the University of Pittsburgh, where he met a member of the Mellon family, the founders and supporters of the Hôpital Albert Schweitzer in Deschapelles, Haiti. The Schweitzer Hospital was a modern facility, at least by Haitian standards, and Paul decided he would try to get a job there.

In the spring of 1983, when he was twenty-four years old, Paul made his first trip to Haiti. When he stepped off the plane into the heat and chaos of Port-au-Prince, he had a thousand dollars in his pocket and had taught himself a little Creole. Little did he know that this was the start of a relationship with all things Haitian that would profoundly and permanently change his life. With high hopes that his Mellon contact would help him secure a job at the Schweitzer Hospital, he immediately set out for Deschapelles, seventy miles north of Port-au-Prince, and applied for a job at the hospital. But that didn't work out either; again disappointed, he headed back to Port-au-Prince. I always have a little chuckle when Bill Clinton introduces Paul to a crowd and says that when he asked Chelsea if she knew who Paul Farmer was, she replied, "Of course, Dad, he is our generation's Albert Schweitzer."

So instead of finding work in Africa, his first choice, or at Schweitzer Hospital, his second choice, Paul took a volunteer position at a small organization called Eye Care Haiti. Based in Port-au-Prince, Eye Care Haiti has mobile outreach clinics in rural areas, and Paul was sent to Mirebalais, a town in the Central Plateau. He worked in a clinic only a few miles from the site where, thirty years later, Paul and his Partners In Health colleagues would build a three-hundred-bed, state-of-the art, Harvard-affiliated teaching hospital.

In retrospect, 1983 turned out to be a year that would have long-lasting significance for Paul, not only because it marked his first trip to Haiti, but perhaps even more importantly, because of several lifelong relationships he formed during this time. The chance meeting of Paul Farmer and Ophelia Dahl at a dilapidated building in Mirebalais, where they were both volunteering at the eye care clinic, was the start of an extraordinary friendship that has endured for over thirty years and a long-term partnership that, in time, would change the face of the global health world and bear fruit in the lives of millions of poor people Paul and Ophelia will never meet on this earth.

Ophelia was eighteen years old; her father had shipped her off to Haiti from her home in England to do some volunteer work that would broaden her horizons. Her father, Roald Dahl, was a much-celebrated author, and her mother was Patricia Neal, an Academy Award–winning actress. Ophelia had a complicated family life, and the time away from home was an opportunity for her to gain some independence and figure out what the future might hold for her. As chronicled in some detail in *Mountains Beyond Mountains*, the first incarnation of Paul and Ophelia's relationship was a serious romantic involvement that spanned almost a decade.

The backdrop for the development of their relationship was the poorest country in the Western hemisphere, politically unstable from years under the Duvalier dictatorship, which took a terrible toll on practically every aspect of life in Haiti. Ophelia found Paul, five years her senior, to be an intriguing and attractive person. She liked his outgoing personality and was impressed by his serious efforts to understand Haiti from an anthropological perspective and his passionate ideas about how to change the circumstances of the poor. For his part, Paul liked Ophelia's sometimes bawdy sense of humor and her willingness to engage in deep conversation, and he was no doubt taken by her beauty and innocence. Young and without any responsibilities, they began to spend a lot of time together, exploring Haiti and trying to interpret their shared experience.

Ophelia returned to England for a time, thinking—no doubt influenced by Paul—that perhaps she would become a doctor too. She would eventually return to Haiti in the summers to work with Paul on projects in Cange and joined him in Boston when Paul started medical school at Harvard. They were a committed couple who got along well, and for several years they envisioned a life together organized around the shared goal of working to improve the lives of the destitute poor. But Ophelia would eventually turn down Paul's proposal of marriage when she realized that she was not cut out for a life with a doctor whose total dedication to the poor would always come first. Paul was devastated when Ophelia decided against marrying him, and Ophelia was sad too, but she was wise enough to know that in the end, they would both be miserable. They parted for some time after their broken engagement, but while Ophelia knew she could not make a life with Paul as his wife, she very much wanted a friendship with Paul, for she believed in him and in the work he was doing. Over time, Paul and Ophelia's relationship developed into an enduring friendship and, eventually, a legendary partnership that finds its expression in serving the poor through their work together at Partners In Health, where Ophelia served as executive director for twenty-five years until 2015, when she turned the day-to-day operations over to their esteemed colleague and friend,

Dr. Gary Gottlieb. Ophelia, ever dedicated to the world's poor, still serves full-time at Partners In Health as chair of the board of directors.

In her 2006 commencement address at her alma mater, Wellesley College, Ophelia told the graduates something of her experience working with Paul to start Partners In Health: "We didn't have a budget or a strategy. . . . As the number of patients and their ailments grew, we expanded the services, raising more money until the clinic became a hospital, the classroom a school, and the entity we referred to as 'the project' became Partners In Health. . . . So feel free to start very small, but allow yourself to imagine very expansively."[4]

Starting Small, Imagining Expansively

And that is just what Paul did: he started small but was imagining expansively. After his volunteer work at the eye clinic ended, he traveled around Haiti, hitchhiking or catching a ride on one of the brightly painted Haitian tap-tap buses, taking it all in, quickly forming opinions, imagining how things could be different. He knew he was seeing firsthand the "social inequality" he had read about in textbooks at Duke. As he told anthropologist Barbara Rylko-Bauer in an interview, "By the time I got to Haiti, the idea of being a dispassionate neutral observer was dead to me."[5]

While working as a volunteer at a hospital in Léogâne, he witnessed a horrible medical crisis that awoke in him an intense sense of moral outrage followed by a strong motivation to act.[6] One evening, a young pregnant woman, desperately ill with malaria and in severe respiratory distress, was brought into the hospital. The doctor told the woman's sister that the woman needed a blood transfusion to save her life and suggested that the sister go to a blood bank in

Port-au-Prince and buy the blood needed to save her sister's life. But her family did not have the money. Paul tried to raise some money by begging around the hospital complex, but he could only come up with fifteen dollars, which was not enough to cover the cost of the blood *and* transportation to Port-au-Prince. Paul stood with the devastated family and the hospital staff, helpless, as the woman and her unborn baby died. The woman's family thanked Paul for trying to help, which only made him feel worse. But it was something that the woman's sister said to him that just crushed him. "This is terrible. You can't even get a blood transfusion if you are poor." Sobbing, she kept repeating, "*Tout moun se moun, tout moun se moun,*" which in Haitian Creole means "We are all humans, we are all humans."[7]

In what would become his standard practice over the years, Paul's outrage drove him to action. He decided to try to help the hospital build its own blood bank, so that a tragedy like this would never happen again. Thus began Paul's first foray into fundraising. In the years ahead, he would raise untold millions of dollars, but this first attempt, through asking family and the parents of some friends from Duke, netted a few thousand dollars. He enthusiastically and boldly went to the hospital leadership and told them he had raised the funds to build a blood bank at their hospital. They probably thought he was a bit cheeky, as well as obviously clueless about the way things work, when he told them that he wanted the blood bank to be free of charge. After they let him know in no uncertain terms that the blood bank would not be free, he left with a curt good-bye, filled with outrage. This was a watershed moment for Paul. Standing outside the hospital that had just dismissed him, he made a promise to himself: *I am going to build my own hospital where the poor receive good health care free of cost.* To say that he made good on his promise is the understatement of all time.

Before his time in Léogâne, Paul had briefly connected with Fr. Fritz Lafontant, another religious person who would come to figure prominently in his personal history. Fr. Fritz, an energetic and determined Anglican priest, and his charming wife, Yolande, fondly called Mamito, had settled in the Central Plateau, where they ran a medical clinic in Mirebalais and some modest programs in a squatter settlement in Cange, a village about twelve miles from Mirebalais. Twelve miles sounds nearby, but the roads were not paved, so it was a rough and bouncy drive over dirt roads that could take hours, especially in the rainy season when the river flooded. The lives of the people in Cange had been destroyed when their land was flooded by a well-intended development project gone awry—the building of a hydroelectric dam in the 1950s. Paul has often remarked that he thought he had grown up poor until he got to Haiti and saw what real poverty was like. When the valley flooded, the people of Cange lost their homes and their livelihoods as farmers: their lives were utter misery, with crude lean-tos for housing, no stable food or water source, and virtually no medical care or educational or job opportunities. They simply had no access to the goods and services that make human flourishing possible.

Fr. Fritz and Mamito welcomed Paul, seeing in him great promise and quickly realizing that his drive and energy would make him a good partner in their work. They were solidly behind his idea of building a hospital where the poor could receive good medical care free of charge. Paul's first assignment as a volunteer was taking vital signs at their medical clinic in Mirebalais. Like all of the other clinics Paul had visited around Haiti, the clinic was a dismal place lacking most, if not all, of the tools of the trade necessary to make it a decent health care center. During his time there, Paul mostly learned the way a medical clinic should *not* operate. But this did not depress him; instead, it motivated him to do what was necessary to improve the situation.

With the blessing of Fr. Fritz, Paul turned his attention to Cange and began to formulate modest plans to build a health care system there that would include other social supports like feeding the hungry, clothing the naked, and giving clean water to the thirsty. He started planting trees, as the land had been denuded, its forests chopped down for cooking fuel. If you go to Cange today, you will see a beautiful, lush green valley, filled with tall trees planted by Paul some thirty years ago. Paul stayed for the rest of the year, waiting to hear from medical schools, and it was Fr. Fritz who handed him his acceptance letter from Harvard Medical School. Paul briefly toyed with the idea of staying in Haiti, where the work was so immediate and compelling, but Fr. Fritz insisted otherwise, explaining to Paul that his medical training would make him much more useful in the long run. And so, in the fall of 1984, Paul left Haiti for Cambridge, Massachusetts, to begin a joint MD-PhD program.

The Harvard-Haiti Pilgrimage

One might say that during Paul's time as a student at Harvard Medical School, his mind was in Massachusetts but his heart was in Haiti. For many years, as he completed his education and residency, he shuttled back and forth between Haiti and Harvard, often leaving Boston on Thursday, making the ten-hour trek to Cange via Miami and Port-au-Prince, and returning late on Sunday night. Paul enjoyed the academic life, his grades were excellent, and Haiti was a perfect training ground for the kind of medical work he planned to do. But this was yet another "negative contrast experience," for in a matter of hours, he bounced between two opposing realities that revealed the striking differences between the "haves" and the "have-nots" of this world. At Harvard, Paul was surrounded by people following their dreams, exercising their personal agency, taking advantage of endless opportunities, and—of course—taking for granted a safe place to live, endless food choices, and access to modern medical care. In Haiti, Paul was surrounded by people scrambling to eke out a marginal existence, never even daring to dream of exercising their personal agency, instead weeping with shame because they were unable to come up with a few dollars to pay the school fees for their children. Their personhood was truncated: they lived in leaking, one-room lean-tos, worried daily about finding something to eat and safe water to drink, and stood in the beating sun for hours waiting for entry into a subpar medical clinic that was likely not to have the diagnostics or medications needed for treatment.

Paul handled the back-and-forth pretty well. He was a serious student, intellectually gifted, and he applied himself to his studies in medicine and anthropology, motivated by the expectation that he would apply the training and skills he was receiving to help improve the lives of the poor Haitians with whom he was now living and working. He liked Boston well enough, but Haiti was his "True North" where he felt most at home. The progress he saw unfolding on his projects was rewarding, and he had begun to strongly identify with the Haitian people. By nature, Paul has a cheerful disposition, and this helped a lot, but the ongoing Haiti-Harvard commute was not easy. Sometimes it took its toll, and a quiet anger would simmer right underneath the surface when he encountered yet another example of terrible injustice.

Paul struggled to understand why the poverty and suffering surrounding him made what the Haitians call "stupid deaths" a way of life for billions of poor people. "Stupid deaths," like the pregnant woman at the hospital in Léogâne, are a common occurrence among poor people who have treatable medical problems but no access to modern medical care. In 1997, Paul wrote an article in *America* magazine entitled "Listening for Prophetic Voices in Medicine," in which he made the claim that "the experiences of those who are sick and poor remind us that inequalities of access and outcomes constitute the chief drama of modern medicine."[8] In the article, he describes the treatment program of two of his patients: a young woman with advanced AIDS and a thirty-five-pound nine-year-old boy with tuberculosis who quietly asked him, "Am I going to die?" Both were desperately sick the first time Paul saw them in clinic, and had they not encountered Paul, both would surely have died— "stupid," unnecessary deaths way before their time. Instead, they both recovered. Why? Because they received the same treatment they would have been given had they lived just a short plane ride away in Miami. His anger creeps out when he adds: "If you'll permit me a bit of sarcasm, it is almost as if they had a treatable infectious disease."[9]

Reading the work and insights of liberation theologians helped Paul understand that "poverty is not some accident of nature but the result of historically given and economically driven forces."[10] Liberation theology's idea of making a preferential option for the poor caught his attention and made sense to him, and he began to think about what this meant and how it could apply to his work and his long-term goals. As his life in Cange took root, Paul began to view the world from below, listening and learning from the poor people he was living and working with, many of whom have become his friends. In time, it would become clear to him that making a preferential option for the poor in health care would be the organizing principle for his life's work and the way in which he would evaluate the success or failure of all he attempted to do.

His ideas about religion were also changing during this time: "The fact that any sort of religious faith was so disdained at Harvard and so important to the poor—not just in Haiti but elsewhere, too—made me even more convinced that faith must be something good."[11] Paul admired the faith of the people he was meeting in Haiti and their belief that God loves the poor and is on their side. He agreed with liberation theology's blunt rejection of the suggestion that those who are poor will get their reward in heaven and must endure crushing poverty now because it is God's will. He believed in the corporal works of mercy and tried to put them into action on a daily basis. This period was a sensitive time for Paul on the spiritual level, as he came to see the Crucified Christ in the daily lives of the poor. He thought that the liberation theologians' edgy claim—"You want to see where Christ crucified abides today? Go to where to poor are suffering and fighting back, and that's where He is,"[12]—was right on the mark.

Weapons of Mass Salvation

In December of 1983, Paul had made a quick trip from Haiti to Boston for two purposes: to interview for medical school, and to visit Project Bread, a charity that gave away bakery equipment, in hopes of acquiring an oven to build a bakery in Cange. During the interview process at Harvard

Medical School, Paul met Jim Kim, who was also interviewing for medical school. Jim is a Korean American, raised in the Midwest. He had just graduated from Brown University, and he too was idealistic and ambitious. These two young men sensed that they had much in common and formed an intellectual and emotional bond that has endured for decades: "twin sons of different mothers," as Jim likes to say. Jim learned about Paul's work in Haiti, wanted to join the effort, and would become one of the founders of Partners In Health. Today, Jim serves as the President of the World Bank, where he is one of the world's most influential advocates for the poor. He and Paul have remained the closest of friends, often collaborating, always allies in the fight for the rights of the poor.

Paul's visit to Project Bread to ask for an oven for Cange ended up having other long-term consequences as well, for this led to a meeting with a man named Tom White. Tom was in his early sixties and had amassed some wealth from his successful construction company. He was a tender-hearted man, concerned about the plight of the less fortunate, and a Catholic to whom the corporal works of mercy mattered. Tom had already told his family and friends that he intended to give away his entire fortune and planned on dying a poor man. He was an anonymous donor to Project Bread, and had read an essay Paul had written in a Harvard publication. He liked the article and asked the folks at Project Bread for an introduction. Paul met with him in Boston a few times, and they hit it off. Tom liked Paul's passion and pluck and his big dreams to help the poor.

In the summer of 1985, Paul picked Tom up at the Port-au-Prince airport in his battered truck, and they made the long, bumpy trip out to Cange. Paul showed Tom around and told him of his plans for putting in place a health care system that would include a clinic that provided first-rate medical care. He also shared his ambitious plans to build up the community with a school, a church, an adequate food supply with decent nutrition, and a safe water and sanitation system. Tom was horrified by the abject poverty he saw, especially the hungry children, and wanted to help. Although Paul would surely have persevered until he found another avenue for support, it was Tom White's generosity that, in a very concrete way, gave Paul his start. And for the next twenty-seven years, until the time of his death, Tom never wavered in his support. When he died at ninety years old, he had indeed achieved his goal of dying penniless (after having provided for his family), having given, with great joy, much of his fortune to Partners In Health.

Partners In Health

For about three years, from 1984 to 1987, Paul, Jim Kim, Tom White, and Ophelia Dahl formed a hard-working, committed but still informal coalition. Based in Boston, they worked together on a variety of projects in Cange that were going well. Tom was providing significant financial assistance, as was the Episcopal Diocese of Upper South Carolina, which formed a partnership with Fr. Fritz's parish in Cange. In 1987, Tom put up a million dollars to start a nonprofit organization to formalize and advance their work in Haiti. Paul, Ophelia, Tom, Jim Kim, and Todd McCormack, Paul's friend from Duke, who was now living in Boston, joined forces as cofounders. Many intense conversations took place, sometimes into the wee hours, about the moral implications of working among the poor and the philosophy and model they would create for their organization. They decided to call their fledgling organization Partners In Health, and borrowing from liberation theology, they declared that its mission would be to "provide a preferential option for the poor in health care." It is not surprising that Catholic theological thought, and political, moral and ethical social teachings resonated with the group; Paul, Tom, and Todd were practicing Catholics, and Jim had been greatly influenced by his mother, a philosopher and theologian who holds a PhD from Union Theological Seminary. The founders wanted the organization to be "at its root . . .both medical and moral," to "[strive] to achieve two overarching goals: to bring the benefits of modern medical science to those most in need of them and to serve as an antidote to despair."[13] They committed themselves to three things: First, *to make common cause with the poor* by accompanying them, at the practical level, in their daily struggles and suffering, and by eliciting their experience and views and incorporating these views into all observations, judgments, and actions. Second, *to do whatever it takes to make the changes necessary to remedy the suffering of the poor* just as they would do for a member of their own family—always refusing to accept lower aspirations for treatment and care for the poor and deeming arguments like "it's not sustainable" (often code for "the lives of the poor are not worth as much as the lives of the rich") as completely unacceptable. Third, *to work to change the entire situation that has given rise to the poverty* by becoming deeply involved in advocacy and policy work on the national and international levels, challenging—in word, action, and outcomes—conventional thinking and accepted policies and practices in the global health world, the academy, and corridors of power such as the United Nations and the US Congress. Their goal was to create an organization that would, in the words of Gustavo Gutiérrez, "[correct] the injustice of poverty by both accompaniment of the locally poor and advocacy of the globally powerful."[14]

It was a heady time, filled with exciting possibilities, and the creative dynamic within this committed group further fueled their motivation. Even then, starting small, they had big plans and were imagining expansively. Even so, it is unlikely that any of the cofounders could have imagined that 30 years later, Partners In Health would have grown to be an internationally recognized organization delivering high-quality health care to over 8 million of the poorest people in the world at 120 hospitals and clinics in 11 countries around the globe, and that their vision, enduring commitment, and hard work would have brought about dramatic and large-scale improvements in the lives of tens of millions of poor people, often defying what many health care experts say is possible in resource-poor settings.

CHAPTER THREE

Coupling Inquiry and Implementation

Making a Preferential Option for the Poor in Health Care

There was a rich man who was dressed in purple and fine linen and who feasted sumptuously every day. And at his gate lay a poor man named Lazarus, covered with sores, who longed to satisfy his hunger with what fell from the rich man's table; even the dogs would come and lick his sores. The poor man died and was carried away by the angels to be with Abraham. The rich man also died and was buried. In Hades, where he was being tormented, he looked up and saw Abraham far away with Lazarus by his side. He called out, "Father Abraham, have mercy on me, and send Lazarus to dip the tip of his finger in water and cool my tongue; for I am in agony in these flames." But Abraham said, "Child, remember that during your lifetime you received your good things, and Lazarus in like manner evil things; but now he is comforted here, and you are in agony.

Besides all this, between you and us a great chasm
has been fixed, so that those who might want to
pass from here to you cannot do so, and no one can
cross from there to us."

Luke 16:19-26

I believe we will be judged by how well we do
among the destitute sick. Strategies designed to pro-
long life into the tenth decade will flourish in the
affluent world but only if general anesthesia puts
all souls to sleep will history judge us by the longev-
ity of the affluent. No, discerning judges will look
instead for falling life expectancies among the poor,
wherever they live.[1]

Paul Farmer

Making Common Cause with the Poor

In 1990, when he was thirty-one years old, Paul graduated
from Harvard University with an MD and a PhD in medical
anthropology. He and Jim Kim, one of his cofounders at
PIH, were admitted to the prestigious residency program at
Boston's Brigham and Women's Hospital, where they were
given permission to share one residency position and divide
their clinical training time between Haiti and Harvard.
Paul's revised doctoral dissertation, *AIDS and Accusation:
Haiti and the Geography of Blame,* was accepted for publication by the University of California Press, beginning
what would become a prolific writing career. But what held
his interest and motivated him was the way his medical and
anthropological training expanded his potential to make a
preferential option for the poor in health care.

Paul's education at Harvard was, by any standard, first-rate, but his "seat-of-the-pants" education in Haiti was first-rate too, for as we all know, much, if not most, of our learning does not take place in a classroom. The combination of two very different "classrooms"—the hallowed halls of Harvard University and an impoverished squatter settlement in rural Haiti—was no doubt disquieting. Yet Paul's Harvard/Haiti experience made possible the very best outcome one could hope for: now his deep compassion for the suffering of others was coupled with top-notch clinical training and the sharp interpretive eye of an anthropologist. He now possessed both the will and the skill to translate the lofty moral imperatives he embraced into a formidable plan of action.

During his Harvard-Haiti residency years, Paul's personal life was changing too. In 1996, he married Didi Bertrand, a lovely woman he met in Haiti. He had known Didi and her family for many years before their romantic relationship began about two years prior to their marriage, when, in Didi's words, he began "courting her." Didi grew up in Cange, where her father, Prosper, is the schoolmaster. Sadly, Didi's mother died of cancer when Didi was in her teens. As the oldest child in the family, she assumed responsibility for her three younger siblings with a fierce love that continues to this day. Didi is a tall and elegant woman, quite beautiful with a lovely smile. She is quiet and a careful listener, strong-willed and dedicated to her people and her country, and not afraid to stand up for what she believes in. Their marriage was celebrated by thousands of well-wishers in both Haiti and Boston. From the start of their relationship, she and Paul shared a commitment to a preferential option for the poor; indeed, these very words were engraved inside their wedding bands. Two years after they married, they joyfully welcomed a daughter, Catherine.

Partnerships and Friendships

In the decade following the founding of Partners In Health, Paul took the concept of a preferential option for the poor and, as the saying goes, ran with it. During the years Paul was in medical school, PIH moved forward in Haiti and formed a sister organization called Zanmi Lasante (Haitian Creole for Partners In Health), the first of many sister organizations it would form in countries around the world. Things were progressing in Cange on a small scale, although to the people whose lives were radically improved, the changes probably seemed fantastic. By 1989, there was a bustling compound that included the Clinique Bon Sauveur, a big school, a pretty church, staff offices, and a guesthouse. Meals were being provided to thousands of people, and many lean-to shacks had been replaced with small houses with tin roofs. The PIH model for health care delivery was taking shape: a big army of health care workers from the local community was being trained, and health outcomes were improving for the whole community. PIH was the first health care organization in Haiti to treat patients with HIV/AIDS, ignoring the critique that it was "not feasible" or not "cost-effective" and achieving excellent results.

From the start, the global health equity model Paul envisioned was innovative, ambitious, and complex. His goal was to link research, teaching, service, and advocacy together, bringing diverse organizations and individuals together with each activity informing the other with an outcome that would strengthen and improve the whole effort. From the beginning, he also realized that "no one can promote justice on their own,"[2] and he instinctively understood that with "rare exceptions, all of your most important achievements on this planet will come from working with others, or in a word, partnership."[3] To that end, Paul and his colleagues at PIH and Harvard have worked tirelessly over the last thirty years to build long-term, deeply committed partnerships with a wide variety of institutions and individuals. They have partnered with the world's leading medical and academic medical centers, and have actively engaged with powerful public and private foundations and global institutions, sometimes working as partners, and have advocated within these institutions when necessary. They have harnessed the goodwill of thousands upon thousands of caring and generous people to support their work through philanthropy. They sought all of these partnerships with the aim of garnering the necessary support and resources to respond to the needs of the suffering poor and attack poverty at its root causes to create systematic structural change. Blessed with contagious confidence, Paul has been extraordinarily successful at convincing others to invest in his moral vision.

Paul would be the first to say that he has accomplished nothing on his own and that he owes much of who he is, how he thinks, and certainly what he has accomplished to the partnerships and relationships that have graced his life. Among these relationships, three priests figure prominently in Paul's spiritual formation, his professional writings, and his public presentations. The first of this diverse trinity has already been mentioned: the noted Peruvian theologian Fr. Gustavo Gutiérrez, OP. The second, whom Paul would meet in his early years in Haiti, is Jean-Bertrand Aristide, who in 1990 would become Haiti's first democratically elected president. And the third is an American diocesan priest, Fr. Jack Roussin, who was the pastor at St. Mary of the Angels parish in Roxbury, Massachusetts, where Paul lived when he was a student at Harvard Medical School.

Fr. Gustavo and the PIH-Liberation Theology Model

As mentioned earlier, Paul first encountered Fr. Gustavo's writings when he began to read liberation theology at Duke; he studied them further in Haiti, where "it was the patient, scholarly work of Gustavo Gutiérrez that helped me make sense of the poverty I saw around me. . . ."[4] He began to understand and name the social and economic forces that caused the crushing poverty and suffering surrounding him. Paul would go on to borrow heavily from liberation theology in his own writing and work. Key concepts from liberation theology such as structural violence, social analysis, solidarity and advocacy, accompaniment, giving voice to the suffering poor, and the "see, judge, act" methodology shaped the "PIH-Lib Theo Model" or "option-for-the-poor medicine,"[5] as Paul calls it. And Fr. Gustavo's thinking has shaped Partners In Health since its earliest days, when its founders committed themselves to make liberation theology's organizing principle, the preferential option for the poor (the "O for the P" in PIH circles), the heart of their work in health care. I don't think it is an overstatement to say that liberation theology is part of the reason why Paul's approach to global health delivery differs significantly from that of many traditional global health experts.[6]

Paul has often publicly expressed gratitude to Fr. Gustavo for his role in influencing the PIH mission and model. However, Fr. Gustavo's influence on Paul's life extends beyond the academic and professional, for Fr. Gustavo has also helped to shape Paul's spiritual life. Paul would know Fr. Gustavo only through his writings for about ten years, until they met in the slums of Lima in the early 1990s. This first meeting was the start of a life-giving friendship that has deepened over the years. Although their backgrounds could not be more different, they have much in common, including an enduring love for a God who sides with the poor and an audacious moral imagination that dares to dream of a world without poverty. Both men have lived among the poor and forged unusual career paths as academics and practitioners committed to integrating theory and praxis. For Paul, Fr. Gustavo is a mentor and a hero who has influenced him both intellectually and spiritually.

Paul gives lectures at colleges around the United States, and after his talks, hundreds of young people often line up to meet him. It is heartening to see that so many young people want to emulate someone like Paul Farmer, whom they clearly hold up as their hero. But in October of 2011, it was Paul who was excited that he was going to have the opportunity to spend two days with his hero and great mentor, Fr. Gustavo. The occasion was a conference called "Reimagining Accompaniment: Global Health and Liberation Theology" sponsored by the University of Notre Dame.[7]

One evening during the conference, Paul and Fr. Gustavo each gave a talk in honor of the other, moving testimonies to their mutual respect and admiration. Paul's talk was entitled "A Doctor's Tribute to Gustavo Gutiérrez." Before the talk began, Paul made sure that Fr. Gustavo saw that he was wearing a tie embroidered with Dominican shields in honor of Fr. Gustavo's religious order. In the talk, Paul credited Fr. Gustavo with teaching him what he needed to know and do in order to make a preferential option for the poor in health care: "First, real service to the poor involves understanding global poverty; second, an understanding of poverty must be linked to efforts to end it; and third, as science and technology advance, our structural sin deepens."[8] He shared that Fr. Gustavo has influenced his thinking, his life's work, and his spiritual life and closed his lecture with these words: "As long as poverty and inequality persist, as long as people are wounded, and imprisoned and despised, we humans will need accompaniment—practical, spiritual, intellectual. It is for this reason, and for many others, that I am grateful for Father Gustavo's presence on this wounded but beautiful earth."[9]

In his talk, Fr. Gustavo, often referred to as the "father of liberation theology," made his admiration for Paul crystal clear by linking Paul's medical work with the coming of the kingdom of God:

> Correcting the injustice of poverty must involve both accompaniment of the locally poor and advocacy of the globally powerful—the twin tasks that Dr. Farmer undertakes by his very nature. I also wish to place the work of Partners In Health in theological perspective. I find that the way they approach accompaniment of the poor has deep resonance with the message of the Gospel. Jesus bears witness to the Kingdom of God through his words and deeds—and the healing of the sick has a prominent role in his work [and was] a message of life.[10]

These two men, both dedicated to building a world where God's mercy and justice reign, proclaimed their message of hope perhaps most meaningfully in silence at a special Mass held during the Notre Dame conference. As two of the most accomplished and humble men of our times stood side by side at the table of the Lord, eating the bread of life and drinking from the cup of salvation, everyone present was filled with gratitude as the peace that the world cannot give washed over them.

President Aristide and *The Uses of Haiti*

In March of 1991, Paul wrote an article that appeared in *America* magazine entitled "The Power of the Poor in Haiti."

The article, written a month after the installation of Haiti's first democratically elected president, Fr. Jean-Bertrand Aristide, has a cautiously hopeful tone and asks a provocative question: "What might it mean to have a government make an option for the poor in a country of poor people?"[11]

By nature, Paul is a gentle person, a lover of peace and harmony, with a deeply contemplative side. He assiduously avoids conflict, sometimes to a fault, even when the best path forward might be to address a conflict and look for a solution. However, as Paul became immersed in all things Haitian, he was forced to confront the fact that to be of service to the poor, he could not ignore the reality that history and "social, political and economic forces drive up the risk of ill health for some while sparing others."[12] He recognized that poverty and oppression are often by-products of these complex social forces and create the "structural violence" mentioned by the liberation theologians he was reading. He saw too that there is a direct relationship between the political economy and the availability of decent public health systems, and he asked two comprehensive questions: First, "how can history and political economy help us understand the skewed distributions of wealth and illness around the globe?"[13] And, secondly, how can we create systematic and durable change that fights the structural violence that hurts the poor?

Engaging with political realities intellectually was clearly necessary, but entering into the rough-and-tumble of politics did not come easily to Paul. The ugliness and discord, the violence and bloodshed, and the abhorrent and callous human behavior he observed were hard for Paul to stomach. At some deep level, exposure to this kind of harshness crushes his spirit; he would always rather be in the clinic seeing patients or planting a garden to bring beauty into the lives of others. But the tumultuous years following his arrival in Haiti, during the fall of the Duvalier dictatorship and the uprising of poor in revolution, made it impossible to avoid the political. It assaulted him from every direction. Furthermore, it was on the minds and tongues of the people he lived among in Cange, and he wanted to stand with them in their fight for social and economic rights. His anger motivated him too as he saw his patients and friends suffer and die needlessly. Three friends around his own age whom he had enlisted to help him with his first health census died because their medical treatment was too little or too late. The illnesses they died from (malaria, typhoid, and puerperal sepsis) were all treatable had they been able to get to a good medical center in time. So Paul schooled himself in Haitian history, and he engaged the political because he knew there was no other way to make a preferential option for the poor. Central to his education in the ways in which history and political economy impact the poor was Jean-Bertrand Aristide.

Paul first heard Aristide on the radio in Cange in 1986; he later made his way to Port-au-Prince to St. John Bosco Church for Mass and to hear Aristide preach the Gospel to his people from the pulpit. Paul spent some time talking to Fr. Aristide after Mass, and the two men, of the same mind in their radical commitment to the poor, formed a friendship and began to spend time together, creating a bond that continues to this day. Paul thought of Aristide as a "liberation theology priest," and he shared many of the same sentiments Aristide preached in his fiery orations:

> Haiti is the parish of the poor. In Haiti, it is not enough to heal wounds, for every day another wound opens up. It is not enough to give the poor food for one day, to buy them antibiotics one day, to teach them a few sentences or to

write a few words. Hypocrisy. The next day they will be
starving again, and they will never be able to buy the books
that hold the words that might deliver them.[14]

For many of the Haitian poor, "the words that might
deliver them" were being prophetically proclaimed by Jean-
Bertrand Aristide, and he soon developed a big following
far beyond the confines of his parish. At least among the
poor, he was "arguably the most beloved figure in the country."[15] His voice had become the voice of the aspirations of
the poor and was a motivating force in the uprising against
the Duvalier regime. On December 16, 1990, a groundswell
of the Haitian poor elected Aristide president of the republic with 67 percent of the vote. Paul was in Port-au-Prince
on election day and described the response: "That night, the
city's silence was broken, not by gunfire, as in previous elec-
tions, but by cries of joy welling up from the poor quarters
throughout Port-au-Prince."[16] For Paul, this victory be-
longed to the poor, many of whom had risked their lives to
line up to vote for a man who had preached a preferential
option for the poor.

If Aristide was beloved by the Haitian poor, he was in
equal measure despised by the military and the Haitian elite.
He was also considered a real problem by local church officials and the leadership of his religious order, who tried
on more than one occasion to silence him. Christian history
is filled with prophets and martyrs who have dared to use
the social Gospel to challenge the status quo, but their out-
spokenness rarely, if ever, goes well for them, at least not in
terms of their reputation and standing in hierarchical circles.
As Cecilia González-Andrieu puts it, "Anyone who claims
theological thought has little to do with real life needs only
remember that prophetic theological work—the work of

interlacing the Christian tradition with the world's pain—is dangerous business."[17] It certainly was for Aristide, when on September 11, 1988, a squadron of armed civilians stormed St. John Bosco during Mass to assassinate him and kill as many parishioners as possible. Aristide was spared—it was not the first attempt to assassinate him nor would it be the last—but thirteen people died and seventy were wounded, and his church was burned to the ground.

Aristide was elected in 1990, and in the early days of his presidency, he instituted programs for adult literacy and primary education and made a commitment to build the kind of public health system Paul championed. But Aristide's victory as the first democratically elected president of Haiti was short-lived; he served only seven months before a bloody military coup forced him out of office. During the brutal coup, from 1991 to 1994, more than three thousand Aristide supporters were brutally murdered, an estimated three hundred thousand were raped, and thousands were beaten, mutilated, and tortured. Chaos reigned throughout the country as vigilante military forces ruled with terror and violence. Many people staggered into Paul's clinic in Cange battered beyond recognition, often near death. Paul too paid a price for his relationship with Aristide and was twice banned from entering the country, sometimes for months at a time. And when he was able to return, things were tense, and he often found himself in threatening situations. Only his useful doctoring skills kept him from harm.

In September of 1994, President Bill Clinton was filled with disgust and fury when shown photographs, provided by Amnesty International, of the hacked and mutilated bodies of the Haitian dead,[18] and ordered US military troops to restore constitutional rule in Haiti. In October of 1994, Aristide returned to serve out the short remainder of his five-year term. The Haitian constitution does not allow successive presidential terms, so Aristide was unable to run again until 2000, when he was re-elected with more than 90 percent of the vote. By that time, post-coup Haiti, the struggling country Aristide was elected to govern, was the most impoverished nation in the hemisphere and one of the poorest countries in the world. Its natural resources were depleted, its forests denuded, its once successful coffee and sugar trade destroyed, and the infrastructure needed to run a country almost nonexistent. With no tax base to generate revenue, no industry to create jobs, and an embargo on aid or cash credits, Aristide simply did not have the resources necessary to run the country, and Haiti had few friends around the world willing to help. His time in office ended badly when, in February of 2004, armed rebels demanded Aristide give up his presidency as rioting took place throughout the country and the rebels took control of many towns and cities and were closing in on Port-au-Prince. While there is some controversy about whether Aristide resigned voluntarily or was forced to do so by the international community, he was airlifted out of the country and would eventually settle in exile in South Africa after a stop in the Central African Republic.[19]

In a book published in 1994 called *The Uses of Haiti*, Paul reflected on how history and political economy can explain the skewed distributions of wealth and illness. Written from the perspective of the Haitian poor (that is, "from below" as the liberation theologians put it), *The Uses of Haiti* is an edgy book, in which Paul does little to hide his simmering anger at the ways in which Haiti has been used and abused by the international community over its two centuries. He presents a well-researched and documented historical overview of the history of Haiti since 1804 when a group of black slaves had the audacity to assert their God-given human dignity and demand the right to self-govern. Terse and well documented, the book critiques the ways in which the Western press has reported and distorted Haitian events, and as Noam Chomsky notes in his introduction, this book "tells the truth about uncomfortable matters—uncomfortable, that is for the structures of power and the doctrinal framework that protects them from critical scrutiny."[20] *The Uses of Haiti* is a passionate book written by a physician "incensed by crimes committed, with utter impunity, against the sick and the poor."[21] Paul admits that he wrote *The Uses of Haiti* "under the influence of this indignation,"[22] however, Paul's passionate and sometimes angry voice only adds to the book's impact and credibility.

Fr. Jack and Multidrug-Resistant Tuberculosis

On December 6, 2001, Dr. Howard Hiatt, noted physician and former dean of the School of Public Health at Harvard, published an editorial in the *New York Times* entitled "Learn from Haiti." In the editorial, Dr. Hiatt describes the health care model designed by Paul Farmer, Jim Kim, and Partners In Health and their success in controlling HIV infections in Cange, Haiti, just as effectively as in America. Dr. Hiatt makes the point that this kind of program "could be replicated all over the world if the wealthy nations chose to provide the financing. The barrier to the use of AIDS drugs for all H.I.V. patients is not some physical or educational impossibility; it is lack of will."[23] Dr. Hiatt went on to say that Partners In Health applied the principles used in Cange in Lima, Peru, and "cured more than 80 percent of patients with drug-resistant tuberculosis—something many tuberculosis experts and even the World Health Organization had thought impossible."[24]

This statement—*Partners In Health "cured more than 80 percent of patients with drug-resistant tuberculosis—something many tuberculosis experts and even the World Health Organization thought impossible"*—is dramatic in its own right because it led to changes in the international protocols for treatment of a disease that was killing millions of people annually, most of them poor. But this statement has an extraordinary backstory too, beginning in the summer of 1984 when Paul arrived in Boston to begin medical school at Harvard and took up residence at St. Mary of the Angels parish in Roxbury, a struggling neighborhood in Boston's inner city. One of the priests at St. Mary's, Fr. Jack Roussin, was committed to the social Gospel and dedicated to helping the poor and disenfranchised people in the neighborhood and beyond. Fr. Jack was young, only in his mid-thirties; he was dynamic, friendly, and inclusive and liked having people around the parish. He sometimes offered housing to students, and Paul, with his work in Haiti, seemed a good fit. Fr. Jack was a great storyteller, and his charismatic personality attracted all kinds of people. He was not afraid to try out bold and innovative ideas, and the parish was growing and thriving. A "mover and shaker" in the Boston community, he was a friend of Boston's mayor, Ray Flynn, who often involved him in city political happenings.

This was a bittersweet time for Paul. He was excited to begin his medical and anthropological training, but he was greatly saddened by the sudden death of his father, Paul Farmer Sr., in July of 1984. Paul Sr. had been playing a pickup game of basketball with his son Jim when he had a massive heart attack. He was only forty-nine years old, and his untimely death left Ginny Farmer a widow with six children. Her youngest child, Peggy, had just left for college, so Ginny decided to return to New England to be near her family and finish her undergraduate education at Smith College.

Paul settled into St. Mary's and was well liked by the others living there, including a newly arrived young priest— Fr. Joe Driscoll, a couple of Harvard Divinity School students, and the sisters on the parish staff. One of Paul's endearing qualities is his ability to form lasting bonds wherever he goes, so it was not surprising when a big contingent of people from St. Mary's came to a talk Paul gave at Boston College almost thirty years later. Paul remembered not only all their names but something of their histories as well, and they stood visiting for a good while.

The breakfast table at St. Mary's was lively, and Paul, sometimes looking like he might have pulled an all-nighter studying, would grab a cup of coffee and visit with Fr. Jack, Fr. Joe, his other housemates, and the staff. He was gone a lot too, off to Haiti whenever he could get away. Joe Driscoll recalls that Paul and Fr. Jack were very close. They were both intellectuals and shared a commitment to serve God's people, especially the poor. Paul attracted all kinds of people to the house, and Ophelia Dahl and other PIHers would often stop by St. Mary's to visit with Paul and Fr. Jack; the talk would inevitably turn to their work serving the poor in the local community and in Haiti. Towards the end of 1992, after sixteen years of service at St. Mary of the Angels, Fr. Jack announced he would be leaving Boston and joining the Missionary Society of St. James the Apostle to fulfill a long-held dream of working among the poor in Latin America. He was headed to Peru as the pastor of Cristo Luz del Mundo Church in Carabayllo, a poor barrio on the northern outskirts of Lima. And of course, Fr. Jack wanted his friends at Partners In Health to join him working among the poor in Lima.

In 1992, five years after its founding, Partners In Health was still a very young organization. Its efforts were focused on Haiti, and almost all of its funding still came from Tom White's extraordinary generosity. Paul, Ophelia, and Jim took Fr. Jack's request seriously and spent some time mulling over the pros and cons of taking on another project. Jim wanted to lead a project and try to replicate the model they had designed in Haiti in a different setting, so with equal measures of trepidation and enthusiasm, they decided to join Fr. Jack in Carabayllo and start Socios en Salud, another PIH sister organization. However, at that time, Peru was engulfed in the violent conflict between the Sendero Luminoso (Shining Path) guerrillas and the Peruvian army. The Sendero movement's goal was radical social transformation through aggressive means, and they had ordered all the nongovernmental organizations (NGOs) working in Peru to leave because "you give crumbs to the people to entertain them and fail to realize that the correct path is that of the people's war."[25] For its part, PIH started small with a few projects, one of which was the construction of a community pharmacy next to Fr. Jack's church that would dispense medicine to the local community for free. The pharmacy project came to an early end, though, when the building was destroyed by a pipe bomb. Here is Paul's perhaps unexpected response to the bombing:

> Shortly after the building was completed, it was destroyed by a bomb. Sendero, everyone said, and the motive was held to be the usual: if we were reformers, patching up the wounds of the poor, we were, in Sendero's eyes, palliatives, delaying the necessary radical transformation of the community.
>
> It seemed cheap to say that we appreciated neither the logic nor the methods of our detractors. Cheap because it's been said so many times, by anthropologists as well as by the pillars of the Peruvian state. Sendero's analysis, though riddled with inconsistency and undermined by arbitrary violence, was less easy to dismiss. We *were* patching up wounds. Such interventions would not, it's true, alter the

overall trends registered in the slums of Lima, settlements growing at a rapid rate.[26]

Although Paul and Jim understood that their work in Peru was not going to create the kind of systematic change that was needed in the long run, they persevered, in part because they had promised Fr. Jack they would. They kept their projects small. However, things changed drastically in the spring of 1995, when Fr. Jack got sick. He exhibited the classic symptoms of tuberculosis (TB): coughing, diarrhea, and night sweats. As he began to lose weight, Paul and Jim insisted that he return for treatment to Boston, where he was placed on the four most powerful drugs available to treat tuberculosis, usually rapidly effective. But the drugs didn't work for Fr. Jack, and less than a month later, he was told that he had only a few days to live. Poignantly, he had one last request. He did not want to be alone when he died, so his friends kept vigil by his side during the last hours of his life. He died on June 9, 1995, at the age of forty-eight. Paul had spent days at a time in the hospital during the weeks while Fr. Jack was being treated and was inconsolable when Fr. Jack died.

Two days after Fr. Jack died, test results revealed that he was resistant to all the first-line drugs that are usually successful in treating TB. Paul and Jim realized that this meant three things: first, Fr. Jack had multidrug-resistant tuberculosis (MDRTB); second, he had contracted MDRTB in Peru; and third, others in Peru would also have MDRTB and were also at risk of death if they were not treated. The tragic death of their beloved Fr. Jack created a certain exigency and presented the group with a moral dilemma. Paul describes their situation like this:

> At Partners In Health, we were faced with more than our own grief. What were our obligations, knowing as we did

that our friend had died of MDRTB acquired in a Peruvian slum? . . .

For years, from Haiti and in the context of the AIDS pandemic, we'd been arguing for a systematic and critical look at the transnational nature of epidemics. We'd been arguing, too, for the remediation of inequalities of access, calling for the sort of pragmatic solidarity that the Haitian poor demanded. Wasn't our friend's death sort of a test case for both our analysis and our convictions? Wasn't it a sign?[27]

Paul already knew a good bit about the clinical protocols for patients with multidrug-resistant tuberculosis. MDRTB is significantly more complicated to treat as patients do not respond to first-line drugs used in the standard TB treatment regimen. Testing for drug susceptibility to identify the particular strains infecting the patients is required, and it is significantly more expensive because of the costs of testing, higher drug prices, and longer treatment regimens. To be blunt, if you lived in a poor country and had MDRTB, your chances of receiving the right treatment were close to nil and your death almost certain. Tuberculosis, as Paul likes to say, "makes its own preferential option for the poor,"[28] for this terrible disease has all but vanished from the wealthier parts of the world because of the availability of inexpensive and effective first-line drugs. Caused by bacteria that most often affect the lungs, TB is highly contagious, spread from person to person through the air. Tuberculosis is curable *if* you are among the fortunate who have access to medical treatment. According to the World Health Organization (WHO), TB remains one of the top 10 causes of death in the world. In 2015, 10.4 million people fell ill with TB, and 1.8 million people died from it. Over 95 percent of these deaths occurred in developing countries.[29]

Once Paul and Jim realized that Fr. Jack had contracted MDRTB from exposure to someone in his local community, they had many intense conversations about the way forward. Finally, they decided they should go to Lima to try to identify and treat what they knew would be many active cases of MDRTB. Working with their colleagues at Socios en Salud, they approached the local health authorities, told them of the problem with MDRTB, and asked for help with developing a treatment protocol. The meeting did not go well. As Paul puts it, the authorities "sharply reminded us that Peru had a model tuberculosis program, as anyone who worked in the field should know. . . . [W]e were sent packing."[30] Information from their visits to the clinics in the shantytowns of Carabayllo presented a very different reality: doctors and nurses told them about many patients who were not responding to the first-line drugs. Many of these patients were tested and a diagnosis of MDRTB was confirmed; others just died because they did not receive the proper treatment.

Paul, Jim, and their Peruvian colleague, Dr. Jaime Bayona, knew that their small organization did not have the critical mass, much less the financial reserves, to take on a problem of this magnitude, so their next step was to make impassioned pleas to the WHO and the US Centers for Disease Control and Prevention (CDC). Those meetings did not go well either, for they learned that the Peruvian officials' position was not only supported by the WHO, but it was the WHO that had promulgated the policies the Peruvians were following. The consensus of these global health experts was that treating MDRTB in the developing world was simply not cost-effective, and thus the limited funds available should be used to treat the larger number of cases that would respond to first-line drugs. In contrast, PIH argued that their data showed at least one hundred cases of MDRTB in just the area of Lima where they were working, and their colleagues knew there were hundreds more cases throughout the city. Since none of these people were receiving the right treatment protocol, they were going to infect others. As PIH asked rhetorically, "Didn't their presence in the midst of a city of six million constitute a public health emergency?"[31] But because they were neither "cost-effective" nor "sustainable," none of the arguments PIH presented to the WHO convinced the officials, so yet again the PIH doctors were "sent packing." This reasoning infuriated Paul then and still does. As he told an audience at the Brown University Medical School commencement in 2016, "Each of these ideas, from cost-effectiveness to sustainability, could be a means of starting conversations or ending them. But in my experience in international health, arguing that treatment is not cost-effective is largely a means of ending unwelcome conversations about the destitute sick."[32]

Such conversations and the refusal to even attempt to treat desperately ill poor people again highlighted the moral problem of steep social inequality, for it meant that in Lima "the second-line anti-tuberculous drugs necessary to treat MDRTB were available on the market but the people most at risk for MDRTB were unable to purchase these drugs in a reliable manner."[33] In other words, MDRTB is treatable if you can afford it, but not treatable if you can't afford it. Paul and Jim decided that they could not be party to this kind of injustice and would go ahead and try to treat the patients themselves, knowing full well that many would consider this a very foolish decision. And indeed, they faced enormous odds with conflicts and problems at every turn. At first, health officials in Lima blocked them from treating the patients and ordered them out of the country, but eventually the local community put pressure on the health officials and they reluctantly agreed to allow a trial to go forward. The medicines were very expensive, around twenty-two thousand dollars per patient, and the financial pressures were constant. Between funding given by Tom White and the drugs that Jim and Paul could beg and "borrow" from the pharmacy at Brigham and Women's in Boston, they were able to cobble together what they needed to treat the first hundred patients. A band of brave and dedicated community health workers accompanied these very sick patients, risking their own well-being through exposure to MDRTB. The regimen took two years to complete, often with debilitating side effects, but in the end the results were excellent, with an impressive cure rate of 85 percent. I was tempted to use an adjective like "extraordinary" to highlight this statistic, but to do so would make it seem as though there is something out of the ordinary about giving a person the medication they require to cure their disease. This is exactly what the expected outcome should be—*except* when you are poor, and then you can expect a very different outcome.

What actually is an extraordinary accomplishment is how a small organization like PIH was able to forge an international change in policy that would save the lives of millions of poor people. The data and outcomes from their pilot treatment program in Peru were able to convince the international medical community, including the WHO, which had "sent them packing" just a few years before, to change their policies on treatment for people with MDRTB. As Howard Hiatt told Tracy Kidder, "Paul and Jim mobilized the world to accept drug-resistant TB as a soluble problem."[34] This policy change did not happen quickly or easily. When the initial results showing the trial's cure rate of 85 percent were published, the medical community did not receive them well; some experts even questioned the integrity of the results from the data Paul and Jim published. But PIH prevailed, and at an international gathering of TB experts in Atlanta on May 10, 2006, new guidelines for treatment of multidrug-resistant tuberculosis were announced, with the goal of increasing the number of MDRTB patients receiving treatment fiftyfold over the next decade.[35] "In the 1990s, many in the TB community were highly skeptical about the possibility of developing effective and affordable ways of treating MDRTB in poor countries," said PIH co-founder Dr. Jim Yong Kim. "These guidelines have settled that argument. Treatment programs should now be scaled up as fast as possible."[36] To help scale up the treatment, Jim led a successful campaign that would eventually reduce the costs of the drugs that treat MDRTB by 95 percent.

Paul and Jim were becoming known and respected in global health circles, and PIH was becoming a major player in the global health world, continuing to advocate for significant changes in national and global health policies and overturning long-held and erroneous assumptions that high quality health care is too expensive and too complicated to be delivered in resource-poor settings.

Sometimes Paul still chokes up when Fr. Jack's name is mentioned. But perhaps he takes solace knowing that Fr. Jack did not die in vain; in some mysterious way, Fr. Jack lives on in the many people whose lives have been saved because they received treatment for the disease that took his life.

The Best-Laid Plans

When Paul turned forty in 1999, his life was pretty settled. On the professional front, he enjoyed an excellent reputation among his peers in the academy and throughout the global health community. He was on track to become a tenured professor at Harvard Medical School and had published two more well-received books: *Women, Poverty, and AIDS: Sex, Drugs and Structural Violence* (coedited with Margaret Connors and Janie Simmons) in 1996, and *Infections and Inequalities: The Modern Plagues* in 1999. He had received a number of prestigious awards, including a MacArthur Fellowship ("genius") grant of two hundred thousand dollars, which he gave to Partners In Health to establish an Institute for Health and Social Justice. He was becoming known in the anthropology world too and in 1999 was the recipient of the prestigious Margaret Mead Award from the American Anthropological Association and the Society for Applied Anthropology. Partners In Health had grown significantly and now had another sister organization, this one in Russia, working in the prisons, where there was a sweeping epidemic of MDRTB. PIH's budget and scope had increased too, as it was one of the recipients of a forty-five-million-dollar grant from the Bill and Melinda Gates Foundation that meant it was able to expand its work significantly.

On the personal front, the Farmer family had arrived at what they thought was a workable long-range plan for their busy lives. When Catherine was a baby, the family lived in Eliot House on the Harvard campus during the academic year. They agreed that they would spend the summers together in Cange, where Didi would be near her family and Paul could continue to practice medicine and work on building a health care system in the Central Plateau. For a time, Didi and Catherine were based in Paris while Didi did graduate work as she too planned to pursue a career in global health equity. But as the saying goes, "If you want to make God laugh, tell God your plans."

On June 1, 1999, Paul received a one-page, typed letter from the Pulitzer Prize–winning author Tracy Kidder. In the note, Kidder thanked Paul for a letter and an article he had sent to him and then got to the real purpose of the letter: "I'd like very much to drive down to Cambridge and talk with you about my idea for a book. . . . I really would like to write this book, but I want to be sure you know what I have in mind and that it's acceptable to you. I think that if all goes well, I'd very much like to join you in Haiti, Peru, Boston and Russia."

Tracy Kidder did indeed join Paul on his travels, trotting around the globe with him for two years. The outcome of Kidder's time and travels with Paul became *Mountains Beyond Mountains: The Quest of Dr. Paul Farmer, a Man Who Would Cure the World.* Released in 2003, the book has sold over 1.5 million copies and has been translated into nine languages. Kidder is a wonderful storyteller, and the engaging book presents a balanced picture of Paul, whom he clearly admires. Paul's motivation for allowing the book to be written was most likely twofold. He probably thought it would be both good for poor people and good for the work of Partners In Health. It has certainly achieved both of those objectives. Whether the book has been good for Paul himself is a question only he can answer. One thing is certain: the publication of *Mountains Beyond Mountains* changed Paul's life in ways he could never have imagined.

CHAPTER FOUR

Mountains, Pathologies, No Cheap Grace

Towards Global Health Equity

Is not this the fast that I choose:
to loose the bonds of injustice,
to undo the thongs of the yoke,
to let the oppressed go free,
and to break every yoke?
Is it not to share your bread with the hungry,
and bring the homeless poor into your house;
when you see the naked, to cover them,
and not to hide yourself from your own kin?

Isaiah 58:6-7

We live in a violently unequal world.[1]

I argue that equity is the central challenge for the future of medicine and global health.[2]

Pathologies of power damage all concerned—and who isn't concerned?—but chiefly kill the poor. These crimes are the symptoms and signs of structural violence. Indeed, when we regard the perpetrators of these crimes from any comfortable reserve, it is important to recall that with our comfort comes a loss of innocence, since we profit from a social and economic order that promises a body count. That is, surely there are direct and causal relationships between a protected minority enjoying great ease and those billions who go without the bare necessities of food, shelter, potable water and medical services. Pathologies of power are also the symptoms of surfeit—of the excess that I like as much as the next guy.[3]

Paul Farmer

Mountains and Pathologies

Paul Farmer was only forty-four when *Mountains Beyond Mountains* was published. It is unusual to have a best-selling biography written about you at that age, for if you are fortunate enough to live a long life, your story is hardly over. Indeed, many of us are just getting started at forty-four. And of course Paul's story certainly did not end in 2003; the following years have been marked by professional achievement, high productivity, and growth in the spiritual life. The publication of Kidder's biography turned Paul into a public figure, a status he certainly did not seek and one that he has not particularly enjoyed, although he wears it casually and mostly takes in stride. There is a strangeness about meeting people who know so much about your professional life, your thoughts and actions, and intimate aspects of your personal life when you know nothing about them. This one-sided familiarity lends itself to assumptions about who Paul is, or what he is like, or how he should act. It also breeds a not-so-subtle set of expectations in areas ranging from the moral to the intellectual and even to personal qualities, sometimes holding him to an impossibly high standard. On occasion, people push the boundaries of polite conduct with inappropriate questions and comments. While Paul seems to manage it well and is unfailingly cheerful and polite in public situations that would drive most of us crazy, there is just no way that it does not takes its toll. But by and large, Paul is unfailingly polite, even in awkward social situations. He especially enjoys spending time with the many young people who admire his work and want to emulate his passion and commitment, and he will spend hours talking with students about their aspirations and plans for the future, and he likes to joke a little, telling them, "You are my retirement plan."

Another Paul Farmer book came out in 2003, this one written not about him, but by him. Like *Mountains Beyond Mountains*, this book changed his life in ways he could not have predicted. Called *Pathologies of Power: Health, Human Rights, and the New War on Poverty*, it is my favorite of Paul's books. It too has been a best seller—at least by the standards of the academic world—selling well over 130,000 copies and becoming a primer in college classes on global health and human rights. It reached a different audience: not the mainstream public who loved *Mountains Beyond Mountains*, but Paul's own tribe—his colleagues and peers in medicine, anthropology, public health, and human rights, and each group had its own set of opinions and expectations. While Paul was already well known in global health circles from the battle he and Jim Kim had fought to change international policy on the treatment protocols for multi-drug-resistant tuberculosis, the publication of *Pathologies of Power* gave him standing as one of the prophetic moral voices of his generation of physicians. As Steven Miles, MD, notes in a review of the book in the *New England Journal of Medicine*: "There are many kinds of gifted physicians: clinicians, researchers, and those who build institutions. Paul Farmer is the rarest of all: a prophet." He calls the book "a profound work" and says it "deserves the widest possible audience."[4] Herbert Abrams suggests that "the book should probably be a textbook in every medical school and promoted by every medical society."[5]

At the same time *Mountains Beyond Mountains* was making him into a "nonprofit celebrity," *Pathologies of Power* cemented Paul's standing in his academic fields as one of the leading voices in health and human rights. Being a "nonprofit celeb" is one thing; being a "prophet" is quite another; and being both, well, these are heady and heavy roles to assume. But Paul is possessed of a humility, an honesty, and a gentleness that serve him well in the face of what might make others vain or arrogant. I believe the source of Paul's humility and gentleness is his spirituality, which is grounded in a willingness to reflect deeply on theodicy—that is, to consider the reality of how evil is active in the world and to dare to ask the painful question of how and why a good God allows the suffering of innocent people. Paul is equally willing to consider challenging questions about the role we humans play in both causing and alleviating suffering.

As should be clear by now, Paul does not avert his gaze from the suffering of others. His pale blue eyes don't miss much as they peer intently and with curiosity out on the wide world from behind his small, round glasses. These eyes stare intently at others while he is in conversation, remain on guard when he is examining and diagnosing a patient, and so often fill with compassion for the suffering of the lonely other. How has constant and prolonged exposure to suffering and injustice affected Paul? What psychological and spiritual toll do these rugged encounters with human

suffering take? It would be foolish to think that he has es-
caped unscathed, and to his credit, he does not pretend
otherwise. He writes poignantly of this toll in the afterword
to *Pathologies of Power*:

> Writing about human suffering runs many risks, and most
> of these risks have been the subject of too much commen-
> tary. But there is also the artifice of packaging something
> so it offends the senses, but not too much. Surely, this too
> is a marker of a lost innocence. I have come to terms with
> the fact that I will never be asked to write, or even reflect
> overmuch on what is described in these pages, because in
> Haiti I am asked to do only one thing: be a doctor, to serve
> the destitute sick. And since none of my patients can pay
> for my services, it is my job, my great privilege, to draw
> attention to the suffering of the poor and to bring resources
> to bear on the problems that are remediable. Most are.
>
>   I contemplate my own loss of innocence with resent-
> ment, sometimes even tearful silence. From whom can I
> demand it back? As Garcia Lorca said, "Things that go
> away never return—everybody knows that."
>
>   Everybody knows that things that go away never return.
>
> Cange, Haiti
March 8, 2000[6]

What effect do this "tearful silence" and "loss of innocence" have on Paul's interior life? He is often asked publicly
if he despairs or loses hope; the answer is always no, and
there are no outward signs that he is disillusioned or bitter.
In fact, he is a hope giver in all sorts of circumstances. In
the epilogue of *The Seven Storey Mountain*, Thomas Merton
makes the claim that our suffering and "solitude will bear
immense fruit in the souls of men [and women] you will
never see on earth."[7] In some mysterious way, Paul's interior

suffering, while quite personal and painful, has followed this path, for instead of harboring bitterness or despair, he has allowed his own suffering to be the birthplace of a deepening compassion and love for all of suffering humanity that indeed bears immense fruit for many people he will never meet in our wounded world.

Epiphany, Metanoia, and General Dallaire

The publication of *Mountains Beyond Mountains* and *Pathologies of Power*, both in 2003, led to significant demands on Paul's time as he became (and remains) a highly sought-after speaker at universities, at medical schools, and for keynote addresses at conferences and meetings. *Mountains Beyond Mountains* has been the common reader in many colleges across the country, and in the first years after its publication, Paul and Tracy Kidder visited many college campuses, always drawing huge crowds. Paul's prophetic voice about the role of physicians and medicine has led to invitations to give the commencement address at dozens of medical schools and universities.

The first time I heard Paul speak publicly was at the Boston College commencement in May of 2005. I had met him in Miami just a few weeks earlier. Paul's commencement address at Boston College was entitled "Epiphany, Metanoia, Praxis: Turning Road Angst into Hope—and Action."[8] It was a terrific speech, filled with religious language and metaphor, as the title suggests, and delivered in a forthright and charming way. Funny and serious, inspirational and challenging, completely suitable for the audience, the address received a standing ovation from the crowd. At one point, Paul shared a little of his own spirituality with the graduates: "I promised I would not try to be an amateur theologian, but what could be more soulful than allowing yourself to be open to epiphany and metanoia and so to know the suffering of others?"[9]

Sharing the dais with Paul at Boston College was Lieutenant-General Roméo Dallaire, who along with Paul was one of three recipients of honorary degrees. General Dallaire was the force commander of the United Nations peacekeeping force in Rwanda during the horrifying genocide in 1994. His unsuccessful attempt to stop the unfolding nightmare, in large measure because he did not receive the troops and support he begged for, is told in his book *Shake Hands with the Devil*. In his speech, Paul spoke admiringly of General Dallaire's courage and compassion and the way in which "the world's indifference to the fate of a large subset of humanity continues to haunt him."[10] Although Dallaire wasn't able to stop the genocide, he couldn't walk away from it either and has waged a "campaign for justice" so that those who died would be remembered and the lessons learned from this terrible violence would not be forgotten. The chance meeting of Paul and the good general at commencement exercises on the campus of Boston College turned out to hold great meaning for Paul, for in the very near future, Paul would begin his own "campaign for justice" in Rwanda.

Never Again

Rwanda is a small, landlocked country in East Africa, about the size of Maryland. In 1994, as the violent and bloody twentieth century drew to a close, the world stood by and watched the most intensive killing rampage of our times take place in Rwanda. On April 6, just days after Christians around the world celebrated the resurrection of the Prince of Peace, a killing spree lasting a hundred days took the lives of between eight hundred thousand and a million people. The genocide was the work of Hutu extremists whose goal was to wipe out the entire Tutsi population, along with moderate Hutus who did not support or join the genocide effort.

Historians mark April 6, 1994, when Rwandan president Juvénal Habyarimana's plane was shot out of the sky, as the official beginning of the genocide, although a complex confluence of political, social, and economic factors had set the stage for the massacre. These violent killings were not spontaneous or accidental, nor were they the result of ancient tribal struggles, for these two tribes had lived together peacefully for centuries. Rather, European colonialism dating to the late nineteenth and early twentieth centuries had sown the seeds of enmity between the two peoples.

In the coming weeks, upwards of one hundred thousand Tutsis sought solace and shelter in churches throughout the country, where they were nevertheless tracked down and brutally killed. Sadly and shockingly, according to some accounts by survivors, many victims of the hundred-day genocide were killed by priests, clergymen, and nuns who turned on each other. Many of these churches are now genocide memorial sites, chilling testimonials to the evil that humans are capable of inflicting on one another. Some of the churches have been left intact, just as they were at the time of the genocide, with the blood of the people still on the floors, with personal effects and human bones on display. Signs lettered with the words "Never Again" beg visitors not to forget what happened.

No Cheap Grace

Former president Bill Clinton has often said publicly that his greatest regret from his presidency is that he did not do more to stop the Rwandan genocide. Thus, it is not surprising that he turned his attention and the work of the foundation he created in his postpresidency years to try to make amends in Rwanda. Nor is it surprising that he turned to Paul Farmer and PIH to ask if they would join him in Rwanda, where the Clinton Health Access Initiative was working to bring treatment to people with HIV/AIDS.[11]

In 2005, fully aware of both the deep suffering that marked the lives of the Rwandan people and the extraordinary efforts it would take to rebuild their shattered health care system, Paul and Didi made a radical decision: to uproot themselves from their newly organized lives in Miami and move the family to Rwanda. This choice was not made lightly or naively. A commitment to go live in postgenocide Rwanda among both the victims and the perpetrators could not help but raise haunting questions for which there are no easy, simple, or short answers. Entering the contemporary Rwandan situation demanded the capacity to contemplate the fact that humans are capable of fully turning themselves over to sin and evil while at the same time holding on to the eschatological possibilities of forgiveness and hope. Paul and Didi instinctively knew, to paraphrase Dietrich Bonhoeffer, a theologian Paul very much admires, that there would be "no cheap grace" on the other side of the Rwandan genocide. They understood the complex reality that would undergird their daily lives: living side-by-side both with people who had suffered this unspeakable tragedy and with the very people who had committed these heinous crimes against their neighbors. Only a small percentage of the genocide perpetrators were in prison, and many lived and worked in their local communities. As Paul explained, "For foreigners like me, it wasn't clear who was Hutu and who was Tutsi, and we were not invited to inquire."[12] And besides, Paul will always offer medical care to anyone who is sick and in need of treatment, no matter who they are or what they may have done.

While Partners In Health would work mostly in rural areas, Paul and Didi decided it was best to live in Kigali, the capital city, so eight-year-old Catherine could attend school at Green Hills Academy. It was agreed that Paul would "commute" to his teaching and administrative job at Harvard and spend as much time in Rwanda as possible working closely with the Rwandan government to rebuild their shattered health care system. Didi would focus her efforts on building a national training program for community health workers, a central component of the PIH model. They rented a small house on a quiet street and set up house. An American friend who had been working in Rwanda and was heading back to the United States gave them a dog named Bobby, and Paul, Didi, and Catherine settled into their new routine. It was an exciting time.

On July 18, 1994, three months after the genocide began, the Rwandan Patriotic Front (RPF) led by Paul Kagame, swept into Kigali and took control of the country, ending the genocide. Postgenocide Rwanda was one of the poorest countries, if not the poorest, on the face of the earth. Life expectancy had fallen below forty years, and Rwanda's under-five mortality rate was the highest in the world. Twenty percent of the country's population had been murdered, over one million people were displaced internally or in refugee camps, and every remaining man, woman, and child was affected; most were severely traumatized. Less than 5 percent of the population had access to clean water, the banking system had collapsed, and almost no taxes were collected. There were virtually no public works, and the health and education systems, which had been limited before the conflict, were devastated. Most children were not in school, and fewer than one in four children were vaccinated against measles and polio. Infectious diseases including malaria, HIV/AIDS, tuberculosis, and cholera was rampant, further increasing the death toll. An estimated 250,000 to 500,000 women had been raped, and over half of those raped were infected with HIV, creating a major health emergency.[13] There were few doctors and few operating hospitals and clinics, and much of the population had little or no access to even routine health care. Employment and economic opportunities were almost nonexistent. To sum it up, Rwanda was in shambles.

When Paul and Didi and their Partners In Health colleagues arrived in Rwanda ten years after the genocide, modest progress had been made in some sectors, but there was not yet any semblance of a functioning health care system. As is their practice in each country in which they work, PIH formed a sister organization in Rwanda, Inshuti Mu Buzima (Partners In Health in Kinyarwanda), that committed itself to work in tandem with the Rwandan government and the Clinton Health Access Initiative with the goal of strengthening the public health system in rural and underserved areas of the country. Their work would focus on bringing modern medical treatment to over a million people who had no access to a doctor, a hospital, or desperately needed treatment for HIV/AIDS. The Rwandan Ministry of Health asked that PIH work in three districts, spread throughout the country, selected because they had some of the country's worst health outcomes.

Paul had long before come to the realization that the only way to build durable and sustainable health care systems for the long term was by developing the public sector and partnering with the government, and Partners In Health has always sought to do this wherever they work. However, it is often slow going, as many governments in the developing world do not have the stability, organizational strength, leadership, or resources to mount a comprehensive effort. In this case, Paul was enthusiastic about working in Rwanda because he had confidence in President Paul Kagame's leadership. Five years after the genocide, the nascent government under the direction of President Kagame had advanced a comprehensive development plan called Vision 2020. The plan had an ambitious and overarching goal of building Rwanda into a middle-income country by 2020, and over time reducing and eventually eliminating the need for foreign aid. To help implement their ambitious plan, the Rwandans sought a wide range of development partners, including foreign governments, bilateral and multilateral funders, NGOs, and university affiliations. The Rwandans set out clear guidelines for collaboration, insisting that all partners and organizations work within the framework of the Vision 2020 national plan. As Paul explained, "The policy was clear: NGOs and aid institutions were welcomed if they squared their plans with the reconstruction priorities of the government."[14] While some NGOs protested and criticized the Rwandans for being too controlling, the government remained firm on this commitment, and any organization that was unwilling to work within the plan was not invited to work in Rwanda.

As Paul notes, "Roadmaps such as Vision 2020 are a dime a dozen; implementing them effectively is another matter."[15] But the Rwandans are focused and disciplined, and they persevered despite the enormous obstacles they faced at every turn. While President Kagame is not without critics in the international community, no one can deny that Rwanda's postgenocide reconstruction efforts have been extraordinarily successful and have significantly moved the country forward. Since the genocide in 1994, life expectancy has doubled. Rwanda has achieved some of the most dramatic gains in health and poverty reduction in the world. Ninety-seven percent of infants are vaccinated against ten different diseases, and there has been a two-thirds drop in child mortality. There is near-universal primary school enrollment.[16] Economic growth has been consistent at 8 percent a year, and the GDP has trebled in the last decade. Rwanda is now one of the leading tea producers in the world, and many new, beautiful hotels and ecolodges have been built throughout the country as the tourism sector grows, bringing visitors and income to Rwanda.

Rwinkwavu: A Magnificent Transformation

In an early meeting with Agnes Binagwaho, the dynamic Rwandan minister of health, Paul cheerfully told her, "Give us the worst place you have!" Minister Binagwaho took him up on it and gave PIH an abandoned hospital in the Kayonza District in Eastern Rwanda, about a two-hour drive from Kigali. Paul likes nothing better than a challenge, and this was a challenge indeed. The former hospital, empty since the genocide, was a series of buildings in various stages of disrepair. The buildings had once been used by a Belgian mining company and then as military barracks during the genocide. Bullet holes and hate messages covered the walls. Paul described it this way in the *Boston Globe*: "There were no beds, no patients, no medical equipment. It was abandoned, dirty and scary."[17] There was no semblance even of a functioning clinic in the vicinity and not a single doctor for the two hundred thousand people in the district.

Over time, the transformation of the abandoned site has been, in the words of Ophelia Dahl, "magnificent."[18] Today if you made your way out to Rwinkwavu and turned left onto a dirt road after the gas station in Kabarondo, in a few minutes you would come upon the busy and beautiful hospital complex. You would see a series of buildings that include a pediatric unit, properly ventilated units for tuberculous patients, a sixty-bed maternity clinic with operating rooms for cesarean births, a neonatal unit (the first one in Rwanda), a blood bank, and an emergency room. The lab is fully stocked with the supplies and medicine needed to deliver high-quality health care. Along with primary health services, the hospital offers state-of-the art treatment for tuberculosis and HIV/AIDS.

The grounds of the hospital are filled with beautiful gardens and, of course, a fishpond. Thanks to the generosity of Bill and Melinda Gates, there is a state-of-the art training center that is used by all three PIH sites in Rwanda for ongoing training of staff and community health workers. Housing has been built for visiting doctors and clinicians, and Paul and Didi built a beautiful "friendship house," where they often host friends and guests from all corners of the world.

Finally, a World-Class Hospital

In 2007, Partners In Health took up another challenging project working with the Government of Rwanda to rebuild the Burera District's health care system. Located in the Northern Province of Rwanda, this was one of the last two districts in the country without a functioning hospital or a single doctor, which led to very poor health indicators for the population. Within the first few months, a temporary facility was opened, health care workers were recruited, and medical services were being provided. The longer term plan was much more ambitious, and as 2008 came to a close, construction began on a new 150-bed district hospital in the Butaro sector of Burera.

Given the vitality of the partnership with the Rwandan government, Paul knew this project was an opportunity to build a hospital worthy of the poor, and he threw himself into this effort with abandon. He saw the Butaro hospital project as a chance to right some of the terrible injustice he had witnessed and had long plagued him:

> My 25 years of practicing medicine in the world have taken me through hundreds of clinics and hospitals in 20 or more countries. Some of the most discouraging moments in medical work occur because these facilities are poorly designed or poorly stocked or dirty. Not only are the wretched of the earth forced to endure high risk of premature death (and a high probability of unnecessary suffering), they have to do so in dismal conditions—in clinics that are unclean, unlovely, and staffed, if they are staffed at all, by poorly trained and overworked providers.[19]

The MASS Design Group, led by Michael Murphy and a team of young architects and designers from Harvard, was engaged to plan and design the hospital complex. Paul spent many hours with the MASS team and was insistent that the hospital be built to the highest standards. The architects and designers, all volunteers, spent months in Rwanda in what they called "immersive research," listening to and learning from the physicians and clinical teams, the Rwandan engineers and builders, the patients, and the local community. Incorporating the insights gathered from their listening, the MASS architects created an innovative design for the 65,000-square-foot facility that harmonizes with the local environment. Issues like infection control and planning spaces that mitigate and reduce the transmission of airborne diseases were central to the design. A beautifully built environment was also considered essential because, as Paul argues, "Our patients deserve nothing less." Every room in the hospital looks out on a lovely view, either the stunning mountain range or beautifully designed courtyards.

It is hard to do justice to the beauty of the setting. Perched high on a mountain range surrounded by lush, green trees, the former military base on the Ugandan border has been "reborn as one of the loveliest hospitals on the continent."[20] The public space is restful and incorporates beautiful gardens with fishponds and outdoor areas with generous porches, where patients can sit and rest and visit as they are healing. Using local flora and materials, Sierra Bainbridge, a landscape architect and former project manager of the High Line in New York City, built these gardens with the help of the community, including Paul, who spent many happy hours planting and watering.

The hospital complex offers the same kinds of services you would find in a modern hospital. But the vision for the Butaro District Hospital extends beyond the services provided to the patients. It is a living example of and proof positive that it is possible to build and run a modern hospital capable of delivering world-class medical care in resource-poor settings like rural Africa. On January 24, 2011, Paul stood with President Paul Kagame at the ribbon-cutting ceremony to open the new hospital complex. He was, of course, delighted that his patients now have access to a world-class facility, but he was not completely satisfied because there was so much more he wanted to do.

A Dream Come True: The First Cancer Center in Rural Africa

In 2007, Paul said he wanted to focus significant time and energy on the critical problem of lack of access to cancer treatment in the developing world. The World Health Organization estimates that 70 percent of cancer deaths occur in developing countries, often due to lack of access to medications, equipment, and trained health professionals routinely available in wealthy countries. To Paul, this was a scandal. He likened it to the scandal of lack of access to HIV/AIDS treatment in Africa just a few years earlier, when people said it was too expensive and complicated to treat. Today nearly seven million people in developing countries are receiving treatment for HIV, and Paul was convinced that the same turnaround could be made with cancer.

PIH found a willing partner in Rwanda's Ministry of Health, and together they teamed up with the lofty goal of building a cancer center of excellence at the Butaro Hospital, the first of its kind in rural Africa. Joining the effort were many partners, including the Jeff Gordon Children's Foundation, which provided much-needed funding, and expert oncologists and clinicians from Harvard's Dana-Farber/ Brigham and Women's Cancer Center, who would act as consultants training and mentoring the Rwandan staff. The Butaro Cancer Center of Excellence offers a spectrum of oncology diagnostic and treatment services, including a pathology laboratory, chemotherapy, surgery, counseling, and palliative care—all previously unavailable in rural Africa.

In July of 2012, Paul welcomed former president Clinton, who had helped forge the partnership for this project through the Clinton Global Initiative, to the Butaro Cancer Center. After Paul proudly showed the facility to Clinton and his daughter, Chelsea Clinton, they joined other dignitaries in officiating at the opening ceremony. The opening of this center set a new standard of care for a disease once considered certainly fatal, again proving that it is possible to deliver high-quality health care in resource-poor settings.

Yet Another Dream Comes True: The University of Global Health Equity

For years, Paul has argued that world-class health training should not be beyond the reach of clinicians in low-income countries. He points out that there are over ten thousand academic appointments affiliated with Harvard Medical School alone, and while billions of dollars go into development assistance in poor countries, most low-income countries have no well-funded institutions of higher learning. Paul sees this as yet another terrible injustice, for this means that the health practitioners in poor countries, who are surely as smart and talented as their counterparts in rich countries, are denied the benefit of participating in formal training programs and the opportunity to contribute to generating and sharing knowledge that could benefit the academic discipline of social medicine.

In 2015, Partners In Health, in collaboration with the government of Rwanda and with the financial support of many partners including the Bill & Melinda Gates Foundation and the Cummings Foundation, founded the private, not-for-profit University of Global Health Equity (UGHE). In an interview with Michael Igoe at *Devex*, Paul described the opening of UGHE as "the only terminus" of "a lifelong dream."[21]

Located on the campus of the Butaro District Hospital, the University of Global Health Equity's overarching goal is, according to Peter Drobac, UGHE's executive director, to be an "intellectual hub for the world's best thinkers and innovators in health care delivery."[22] With academic offerings focused on teaching, research, clinical care, and implementation, UGHE will develop global health leaders who have the clinical training and leadership skills to effect transformational change in settings of great poverty. Its first degree program is a master of science in global health delivery.[23] Organized along the lines of an executive MBA, the program is a part-time, two-year course of study for working professionals. Students engage in a learning experience rooted in the principles of global health delivery and receive training in a wide range of fields, including health care management, finance and administration, policy, and research. Classes are taught by local and international experts, including Harvard Medical School faculty, and students learn from a broad network of global policy makers, leading research scientists, community health workers, and social entrepreneurs, offering them opportunities to connect and collaborate with global health colleagues and peers throughout the program. Over the coming years, UGHE plans to expand to add undergraduate programs in medicine, nursing, and dentistry and graduate programs in veterinary medicine and health management.

A Sister and a Brother for Catherine

The years following the Farmer family's move to Rwanda were significant on the personal front as well. Perhaps the most exciting events that occurred while the Farmer family was based in Rwanda were the births of a brother and sister for Catherine. In July of 2007, Paul and Didi shared the news that she was expecting a baby in February. On September 21, when Didi was four months pregnant, she called Paul, who was in Boston teaching, to tell him that a baby girl, only a few hours old, had been brought to the hospital. She further informed him that she had brought the baby home with her and wanted to see what he thought about adopting her into their family. She asked him to return home immediately so they could discuss the matter as a family.

Paul left for Rwanda that evening knowing full well that he was more likely going home to meet his new daughter than going home to discuss whether the family should adopt the baby. Together, in consultation with ten-year-old Catherine, who had long been asking for a sister or brother, the Farmers decided to proceed with the adoption. The fact that they did not test the three-day-old infant for HIV/AIDS until after they had filed the adoption papers with Rwandan government speaks to the kind of people Paul and Didi Farmer are. With great joy, they welcomed this child into their family and named her Elisabeth Grace, a fitting name as she was a quiet and serious baby with a mystical quality about her. Five and a half months later, Didi gave birth to a son, Charles Sebastian. He is the opposite of his quiet and serious sister—wiry, active, and outgoing—and together, they are a charming pair, "Irish twins," as Paul and Didi are sometimes teased. It was a happy and hectic time with the two babies, only a few months apart, taking over the household, and Didi and Paul were thrilled with their growing family.

The work in Rwanda continues to grow and flourish. As of 2018, all told, Partners In Health operates 3 hospitals and 42 health centers in three districts that serve almost 1 million patients and employ 6,400 community health workers. The work in Rwanda has been deeply satisfying for Paul for numerous reasons. First, of course, are the fantastic outcomes for patients. As an example, on December 29, 2013, the *Washington Post* published an article entitled "Paul Farmer's Graph of the Year: Rwanda's Plummeting Child Mortality Rate."[24] The article displayed a graph that showed the steepest decline in premature mortality ever documented. Second, PIH has again proved that it is feasible and possible to bring modern medicine to resource-poor settings on a large scale. "We have shown it can be done," as Paul likes to say. And finally, the achievements in Rwanda demonstrate what can be accomplished through the creation of successful public-private partnership.

Harvard and "the Brigham"

Much is said and written about Paul's medical work with the poor and the fantastic accomplishments of Partners In Health, but to fully grasp the scope and breadth of Paul's life, it is important to understand his rich and productive relationship with Harvard University and Brigham and Women's Hospital, his "paying jobs," as he likes to say with a smile. He serves in leadership positions at both of these great institutions. At Harvard Medical School, he is chair of the Department of Global Health and Social Medicine, a position he assumed when his longtime friend and colleague Jim Kim was named president of Dartmouth College in 2009. At Brigham and Women's Hospital (often referred to as "the Brigham"), the famed teaching hospital affiliated with Harvard, he serves as chief of the Division of Global Health Equity. While Paul has surely brought honor to Harvard University, Harvard Medical School and the Brigham have enabled him to create a platform and programs to actualize his vision of creating an academic discipline around the global health equity agenda. Paul often expresses his deep gratitude to Harvard and the Brigham for their unstinting support, and he is always quick to mention that none of what Partners In Health has accomplished would have been possible without the contributions of his many colleagues around the globe.

Most of the time, physicians who want to work among the poor must do so as volunteers, often using their personal or vacation time for this work. While they might be respected or receive accolades for their efforts, their ability to assist poor people in any comprehensive way is usually limited. Often these good doctors find themselves in situations in the developing world for which they are unprepared because they lack the tools of their trade such as medications and supplies, diagnostic and lab capacity, proper treatment space, and the ability to follow up with patients.

Brigham and Women's Hospital has forged a different model by creating the Doris and Howard Hiatt Residency in Global Health Equity and Internal Medicine. Dr. Howard Hiatt[25] is one of Paul's mentors whom he holds in the highest esteem. This four-year program, the first of its kind, combines rigorous training in internal medicine with the advanced study of public health, and confers an MD from Harvard Medical School and a master's degree from the Harvard School of Public Health. Founded in 2004, this program is creating a generation of dedicated young physicians, trained with both the medical and the nonclinical skills needed to deliver modern medicine to the world's most impoverished people, for full-time work in the field of global health equity.

The Department of Global Health and Social Medicine at Harvard Medical School is the academic and professional home for doctors and clinicians working in the field of global health equity and includes many of the doctors who labor at PIH sites around the world. Dedicated to developing the science of implementation for global health delivery, the department believes that social medicine is at the heart of global health and works to comprehensively advance the academic discipline of global health equity in numerous ways: first, by building academic excellence with a wide range of teaching programs and research projects and supporting clinicians working in the developing world with a focus on implementation and delivery; second, by strengthening models of graduate and postgraduate education through course work, degree programs, and global health and social medicine residencies; third, through advocacy for social justice; and fourth, by coordinating efforts to build an international common agenda around global health equity. In addition to performing administrative duties at Harvard and the Brigham, Paul teaches undergraduates at Harvard College and Medical School. Paul loves teaching and sees it as one of his "vocations." As one might guess, Paul is a very popular professor with undergraduates and medical students alike, and students often line up at his office door to meet with him.

I think it is fair to say that Paul's vision for an academic discipline centered on social medicine will become a significant part of his legacy; and none of what Paul has accomplished professionally and at PIH would have been possible without the support of Harvard Medical School and Brigham and Women's Hospital.

On December 16, 2010, Harvard announced the awarding of the title of Kolokotrones University Professor to Paul, an honor shared by only 26 of Harvard's 12,800 faculty members. Paul is the first to hold this seat, which was established through a gift from Wendy and Theo Kolokotrones (MBA, 1970). In the ensuing years, Paul would get to know the Kolokotroneses well, spending time with them whenever he visited the West Coast where they live. Over the years, they have become good friends. Gracious and modest, Mr. and Mrs. Kolokotrones never fail to bring Paul a big box of his favorite chocolates from See's Candies whenever they meet. Always eager to learn more about the work they so generously support, they continue to provide assistance to Paul's work in many different ways.

Forming close, long-term relationships with people from all walks of life is a pattern that is often repeated in Paul's life, and he enjoys a vast network of devoted friends around the globe. This can partly be attributed to Paul's evident interest in and care for others and his appealing personality. However, I would suggest that there are reasons that go far beyond his attractive personality. I think people are drawn to Paul because through him they become connected to a reality greater than themselves—that is, the possibility of being part of a project that promotes the common good of the entire human race. In a wide variety of ways, Paul encourages his friends to join in the work of helping the poor through "pragmatic solidarity," which he describes as "different from but nourished by solidarity per se, the desire to make common cause with those in need. Solidarity is a precious thing: people enduring great hardship often remark that they are grateful for the prayers and good wishes of fellow human beings. But when sentiment is accompanied by the goods and services that might diminish unjust hardship, surely it is enriched."[26] "Enriched" is exactly the language Paul's friends would use to describe how he has affected their lives.

CHAPTER FIVE

Fighting the Long Defeat

Making Common Cause
with the Losers

Then Jesus cried again in a loud voice and breathed
his last. At that moment the curtain of the temple
was torn in two, from top to bottom. The earth
shook, and the rocks were split. . . . Now when
the centurion and those with him, who were keeping watch over Jesus, saw the earthquake and what
took place, they were terrified.

Matthew 27:50-51, 54
Palm Sunday Liturgy

I have fought the long defeat and brought others
on to fight the long defeat, and I am not going to
stop because we keep losing. Now I actually think
sometimes we may win. I don't dislike victory. . . .
You know people from our background—like you,
like most PIH'ers, like me—we're used to being on
a victory team, and actually what we're really trying
to do in PIH is to make common cause with the
losers. . . . We want to be on the winning team,

but at the risk of turning our back on the losers, no, it's not worth it. So you fight the long defeat.[1]

Paul Farmer

A Call from the Secretary of State

On January 20, 2009, Barack Obama was sworn in as the forty-fourth president of the United States, and the next day, Hillary Clinton, his rival in a long, hard-fought presidential campaign, was sworn in as secretary of state. About four months later, in the spring of 2009, Secretary Clinton called Paul Farmer to ask him to consider having his name placed into nomination for the directorship of the United States Agency for International Development (USAID). USAID is a complex and highly political agency, technically independent but subject to foreign policy guidance from the president, the secretary of state, and the National Security Council. This powerful agency of the US government has primary responsibility for administering billions of dollars in civilian foreign aid throughout the world and works to end extreme global poverty as well as to offer support to US allies seeking to realize their potential by building resilient democratic societies.

Paul was, of course, flattered by this invitation and gave very serious consideration to accepting Secretary Clinton's request to join the Obama administration, thinking carefully about whether his background, training, and gifts were well suited to public service. The prospect of having someone like Paul Farmer lead USAID was exciting to many people in the global health community, and as the news leaked out about the possibility, Paul received encouragement and support from many quarters. One night he came out of a restaurant in Boston and found a group of his students standing with signs and holding a candlelight vigil to show him their support. He spoke with the powers that be at Harvard about the possibility of taking a leave for a high-level political appointment, certainly not an uncommon request, as many Harvard professors have been called to serve in high-level government appointments. After consulting with many advisers and friends, and with some trepidation, Paul called Secretary Clinton and told her that he was open to the prospect of becoming the director of USAID.

All high-level government positions (and there was some talk of elevating this position to the cabinet level) require a confirmation by the United States Senate, so for the next three months Paul fully engaged in the cumbersome process of preparing for a Senate confirmation hearing. The vetting process for a high-level government appointment is intense. There is a lengthy written application that seeks detailed information about every aspect of the candidate's professional background and personal life and actions, including their relational and financial history. This process involves the White House legal team, State Department advisers, and the FBI, who are likely to conduct many interviews with the candidate's family, friends, and business associates. The information gathered is reviewed with a couple of objectives in mind: first, to ensure that the candidate has the appropriate qualifications for the job; and second, to assess whether there is anything in the candidate's background that would be embarrassing to the administration or make it unlikely that the Senate would approve the candidate's appointment. Reviewers were particularly interested in Paul's writing and asked for copies of everything he had ever written. It was quite a scene when he carried two big shopping bags filled with all his books and hundreds of academic articles into the State Department.

One amusing encounter stands out. At one of many meetings in Washington that Paul had to attend for questioning and briefings, the State Department lawyers wanted to discuss some of the measures he would need to take on the financial front should the Senate confirm him. In a very serious tone, one of the lawyers said, "Dr. Farmer, should you be confirmed, you will have to put all your holdings into a trust." Paul paused for a moment and then asked, "What are holdings?" A bit puzzled, the lawyers explained that this refers to "all of your financial investments, including stocks, mutual funds, and bonds." There was another long pause before Paul shared the news that he didn't actually have any stocks, mutual funds, or bonds. He may be the only person ever vetted for a cabinet-level position who had no financial investments.

A team of pro bono lawyers from the prestigious New York law firm Schulte Roth & Zabel assisted with the application process. Headed by Danny Greenberg, a PIH board member and a good friend of Paul's, a team of at least ten people, including lawyers, accountants, and research assistants, worked for several months gathering all the required information. During this time, Paul continued to mull over the prospect and challenges of becoming a high-ranking government official. Reviewing internal information about the workings of USAID, he sought the wise counsel of people familiar with the agency and humbly questioned whether he had the administrative skills to lead a lumbering bureaucratic agency like USAID. Other issues were weighing on Paul too. He didn't know if he could give up the two things he understands as his true vocations: teaching and the clinical care of patients living in poverty. Three months into the process, after more than a few sleepless nights and much soul searching, he came to the difficult decision that he could not in good conscience accept having his name put into nomination for the position. Secretary Clinton, was, of course, disappointed, but Paul was relieved by her supportive and understanding response. However, this is not quite the end of the story of Paul's chances to venture into public service, as a new opportunity to serve in a highly visible role on the international stage was right around the corner.

A Call from the Former President of the United States

Shortly after Paul let Secretary Clinton know that he was taking his name out of the running for the USAID position, he got a call from former president Bill Clinton. Clinton told Paul he had something to discuss with him but had been waiting to see what happened with USAID before reaching out to him because, he said with a little chuckle, he didn't want his wife to get mad at him.

A few months earlier, in May of 2009, United Nations Secretary-General Ban Ki-moon had appointed Clinton as the UN Special Envoy to Haiti. This was Clinton's second tour as a UN Special Envoy, having previously served as the UN Special Envoy for tsunami recovery after the 2004 Indian Ocean earthquake.

In a long conversation with Paul, Clinton explained the work he would be undertaking as United Nations Special Envoy to Haiti and asked if he would consider serving as Deputy Special Envoy, his second in command. UN Special Envoys and their deputies are high-level volunteer positions that come with diplomatic privileges and the imposing title of "undersecretary." For their efforts, both Paul and Clinton would receive the handsome sum of one dollar a year. The terms for these positions are relatively short, usually between twelve and twenty-four months, and do not require a full-time commitment. This appealed to Paul, as it meant he would not have to give up his teaching or clinical practices. With the blessing of his dean at Harvard Medical School, on August 11, 2009, Paul accepted Clinton's invitation to serve as his deputy. At the time of his appointment, Clinton noted that Paul's "credibility among the people of Haiti and in the international community will be a tremendous asset to our efforts as we work with the Government and people of Haiti to improve health care, strengthen education and create economic opportunity."[2]

Clinton's primary charge as Special Envoy was to support the Haitian government's efforts to build economic development that would lead to sustainable social change. Paul believed in the mission. He was convinced, from his many years of work in Haiti and other poor countries, that working with government to build up the public sector was an essential component to lifting a country out of poverty. While he was quick to admit that he was no expert in economics and finance, he understood that economic development leading to job creation was central to a path out of poverty. He was, after all, painfully aware that all the Haitians he knew wanted jobs and income so they could provide their families with housing and food and send their children to school.

Paul and former president Clinton are good friends, and they had worked together on numerous projects through the Clinton Health Access Initiative. Most recently, Paul had turned to Clinton to ask for his help when four consecutive hurricanes devastated several cities in Haiti a year earlier. Clinton's international profile, his grasp of the complex machinery that drives development work, and his extraordinary convening power made him an ideal choice for this assignment. Paul's deep knowledge of Haitian history and culture and his expertise in policy and implementation were huge assets. He spoke both Creole and French and knew everyone in the government's administration. And, perhaps most importantly, because of his long-standing commitment to Haiti and his work with PIH as a physician bringing modern medicine to the destitute sick, he was known and respected by the Haitian people. Together, Paul and "WJC," as his staff affectionately call Clinton, were a formidable team, and there was great excitement as the work plan for the Office of the Special Envoy for Haiti took shape.

As Clinton's deputy, Paul was responsible for setting up the office and the team that would support and implement the mission. In mid-August of 2009, Paul began to spend a lot of time in New York City at the United Nations Plaza. The UN world was not Paul's world, and deciphering the complex UN system was a steep learning curve for him.

Accompanying the Globally Poor, Challenging the Globally Powerful

Founded in 1945 following the devastation of the Second World War, the United Nations was created with one central goal: to bring the world community together to work cooperatively to build and maintain international peace and security. Critics of the UN—and there are many—call it a lumbering, often ineffective bureaucracy. Some complain that its administrative systems, set up seventy years ago, are antiquated and don't work in the contemporary reality. And, of course, there have been many terrible failures, like the one in Rwanda described in the previous chapter. Nonetheless, the UN is a powerful global player that attempts to tackle and respond to the most pressing and complex problems in the world. Paul himself, on more than one occasion, has critiqued one or more of the UN agencies on their policies and practices, but he was nonetheless pleased to join their ranks, even temporarily, and to work from the inside. He liked to say that he thought it was a pretty radical thing to do.

The start-up phase of the Office of the Special Envoy (OSE) was hectic. Paul spent his days building the team that would staff the office and meeting with the directors of the UN agencies to learn more about their work and how the OSE might collaborate to advance the Haiti mission. Within a month, there were about ten staff members in place. Paul asked me to join the team as his chief of staff, and he brought in Abbey Gardner, a policy expert and longtime associate with whom he had worked in Russia. Insisting that the team include Haitians, Paul recruited Nancy Dorsinville, a Haitian anthropologist who had extensive field experience with vulnerable populations. Clinton's office seconded a young attorney, Greg Milne, and the UN seconded the rest of our team, including Jehane Sedky, who had worked for Clinton in his previous role as Special Envoy after the tsunami in 2004. Jehane came from UNICEF and, along with Trina Huang from the World Food Program (WFP), guided us through the UN system and protocols to get the office up and running.

Every day was packed with planning meetings, and there were hundreds of requests to meet with Clinton and Paul from every sector: UN staff, career diplomats, business leaders, academics, the press corps, and Haitian and American visitors from all walks of life, wanting to share their views and asking to participate in some way in mission of the Office of the Special Envoy for Haiti.

Build Back Better

In August of 2008, a series of four successive hurricanes had devastated the Haitian cities of Gonaïves and Hinche in as many weeks, leaving eight hundred people dead and another one million either homeless or badly affected by the severe flooding and food shortages that created a humanitarian and political crisis for months. But Clinton was optimistic about the future. "Last year's natural disasters took a great toll, but Haiti's government and people have the determination and ability to 'build back better,' not just to repair the damage done but to lay the foundations for the long-term sustainable development that has eluded them for so long."[3]

Clinton was well placed to bring about new partnerships among the private sector, civil society, and donors and was willing to use his convening power to help create a more stable and prosperous future for the people of Haiti. His enthusiasm was contagious as he laid out the details and plan for his agenda to "build back better." Paul and the OSE team worked closely with Clinton's team, often making trips up to Harlem, where Clinton's office was located, to discuss and develop our implementation plans.

Paul's first assignment from Clinton was to go on a fact-finding trip to Haiti. The purpose of the trip, as stated in the *Miami Herald,* was to "gauge how best to support the Haitian government in its national recovery plan."[4] Clinton counseled Paul "to focus on two broad agendas: the medical and public health issues I knew best but also the economic issues that influenced who got sick and who did not."[5] The team at the OSE was scrambling to set up the schedule and logistics for the trip and to ensure that all the necessary diplomatic protocols in the formal UN system were in place. We had to break the news to Paul that he was not going into Haiti under the radar and that his freedom of movement and usual mode of transportation—a ride from a Haitian friend or a PIH staff member—would be curtailed as he was now traveling as a UN diplomat. He recounts, "Three weeks later, I made my first trip to Haiti as a diplomat. Such travel was an experience familiar to President Clinton, but was, after hundreds of trips to Haiti, new to me. I moved about in an armored car and in a motorcade; I had a body-guard, a Haitian-American policeman from Atlanta, who politely termed himself 'a personal protection agent.' "[6] Paul was soon on a friendly, first-name basis with the gentleman assigned to protect him, learning all the details of his family situation. And while Paul was gracious and seemed to take it all in stride, he has never really been comfortable with what he called "the heavy protocol."[7]

Six people from the OSE team traveled with Paul on the five-day visit during the first week of September 2009. The schedule was packed full and included a day trip out to the Central Plateau and a helicopter ride to Cap-Haïtien, Haiti's second largest city. In each city Paul visited, he met with the local governmental and community leaders, business leaders, and representatives of NGOs, listening carefully to their concerns and hopes. He spent an afternoon at the presidential palace meeting with the Haitian president René Préval and prime minister Michèle Pierre-Louis and other government officials, many of whom were longtime friends and associates.

An important purpose of this first official trip was to meet with the UN Haiti team. First in command was an old-school diplomat named Hédi Annabi. Mr. Annabi, a native of Tunisia, had a great deal of experience in difficult settings. He had a very formal demeanor and welcomed Paul graciously. Second in command was Luiz da Costa, a Brazilian career diplomat. He too was quite proper but was less reserved, warmer, and more outgoing. After greetings and formalities were exchanged, the conversation took a serious turn. Mr. Annabi and Mr. da Costa (who both eventually invited Paul to call them by their first names) listened intently to Paul's explanation of why Clinton had invited him to serve as his deputy. "Early on, I told Annabi and da Costa that I'd been chosen for the job because of my knowledge of Haiti and of health care, food security, and education."[8] While formality can seem off-putting, especially for Americans who tend towards the casual, it has its benefits, as it allows for difficult topics to be broached and discussed in a civilized manner. This was helpful when the topic of the UN's military presence in Haiti arose. The UN Haiti team numbered in the thousands, and most of them were military peacekeepers whose primary focus was security. The UN leadership team was deeply invested in the presence of the peacekeepers, believing that they could and would stabilize the country with the positive outcome of less violence and greater safety. But Paul had a different view, which he had publicly expressed on numerous occasions, and he was sure that "some faction of the UN leadership surely knew of my concerns about law-and-order approaches to security."[9] Paul's experience working in Haiti among the destitute poor has convinced him that investment in basic social services, not military force, was what was needed. Paul shared his view with Mr. Annabi and Mr. da Costa when he told them that he had "long ago concluded that jobs and services, along with full political participation of the poor, were the best (and perhaps only) way to lessen violence and discord in the places we work."[10] It was a good, honest conversation (and of course unfailingly polite), and the difference of opinion about Haitian politics in no way affected the excellent working relationship Paul forged with Mr. Annabi and Mr. da Costa. At the end of the meeting, Mr. Annabi invited Paul to his home for dinner, and they enjoyed an evening getting to know each other.

Meanwhile, Paul was literally commuting between Boston, New York, Kigali, and Port-au-Prince. Four days in

New York, two days at Harvard teaching, a couple of days in Haiti, back to New York for two days, and then eighteen hours of travel to Kigali to be with his family and to work at the PIH hospital sites. He used the time on the plane to write and keep up on the massive briefing materials the UN continually sent. He kept in touch with Clinton and the OSE office on a daily basis for briefings, to monitor progress and to provide direction and support. Despite the hectic travel schedule, he was in good spirits and pleased to be engaged in high-level policy work that he hoped would benefit the Haitian people, especially the poor, in a positive way.

The next big trip to Haiti was set for the first week of October, when Clinton was convening an international trade mission of private investors. Prime Minister Pierre-Louis boldly proclaimed that "Haiti is open for business"; the slogan caught on and was widely publicized in the international press. An enormous amount of planning goes into an event of this stature—we received a detailed brief on the schedule, the attendees, the press coverage, the intended outcomes, and Paul's role in the event. Paul carefully prepared for the event, trying to educate himself about how the investment world works.

There were high hopes that this gathering would be a major turning point for Haiti. Under President Préval's leadership, the political situation was perceived as stable, and the international community had confidence in the calm and professional Prime Minister Pierre-Louis. On behalf of the president and prime minister, Clinton invited business leaders from around the world to come to Haiti to see firsthand the investment opportunities that were available in a variety of sectors, including construction, textiles and manufacturing, energy, and agriculture. The turnout was terrific: over two hundred potential investors traveled to Haiti for two days of presentations on potential business investments, visits to local sites, and meetings with government officials and business owners. The Haitian government declared the meeting a big success with great potential for building a more stable economic future.

The work at the UN Office of the Special Envoy for Haiti closed on a high note at the end of 2009. The week before Christmas break, Paul took the OSE staff out for a festive holiday dinner. Paul has a way about him that creates community, and the group, none of whom had known each other three months earlier, had become close. There were toasts and funny stories about some of the events of the past few months, and everyone was looking forward to reconvening in January to continue our work "building back better." But once again, even modest progress eluded the Haitian people.

January 12, 2010

At 4:53 p.m. on a Tuesday afternoon in mid-January, a 7.0 earthquake shook Port-au-Prince and wrought destruction and devastation of biblical proportions. Minutes later, Cheryl Mills, Secretary Clinton's chief of staff, called Paul to check on his whereabouts. Paul, Didi, and their children had spent a month in Haiti celebrating the Christmas holidays with family and friends, and Didi and the children had returned to Rwanda just that morning. Paul was spending a few quiet days in Miami with his mother so that he could recuperate from knee surgery to repair a torn meniscus. The plans for a trip to Haiti during that week had been changed; if not, Paul and I would have been at a meeting at the Hotel Montana in Port-au-Prince. It was a sobering moment when word reached us that every single person at the meeting—save those few that were trapped in the hotel's elevator shaft—had died.

In the hours after the earthquake, it was almost impossible to get through to Haiti, so Paul was grateful when Dr. Claire Pierre, a young Haitian American doctor based in Boston, reached her mother in Haiti, who then connected Paul to Prime Minister Jean-Max Bellerive.[11] The early news he had to report was grim. Paul asked what Prime Minister Bellerive knew about casualties. "Thousands?" Paul questioned. Bellerive's reply was frightening: "Tens of thousands. Maybe more. We are in the dark. Tell President Clinton we are going to need his friendship now more than ever. Port-au-Prince is ruined."[12]

Clinton called Paul that evening and asked him to come to New York, where Clinton and the secretary-general would address an emergency UN session on Haiti. Early the next morning, Paul, his mother, and I traveled to New York. Although information was scant, the news feeds had started, and the news and images coming out of Haiti were terrifying. Less than fourteen hours after the earthquake, it was already abundantly clear that this was a massive catastrophe. Paul made his way to a small room at the UN, where Clinton and a few members of his staff were with UN Secretary-General Ban Ki-moon. The tone in the meeting was somber as Clinton and Mr. Ban prepared their remarks for the emergency session. There was agreement that all available resources be focused on rescue and relief. There was a poignant moment when President Clinton asked if there was any way to preserve the bodies of the Haitian dead, so they could be given the dignity of a proper burial. But there was no way, for by the next day, thousands upon thousands of dead bodies were piling up on in the streets of Port-au-Prince. The stench was overwhelming, and President Préval finally had to make the excruciating decision to bury the bodies in mass graves. Among many of the horrible images from those terrible days is one of a huge truck dumping hundreds of bodies into a big hole in the ground—just like a load of dirt.

Paul sat behind Clinton at the UN emergency session. Describing the event, he notes he wasn't sure what role he was to play, but his presence and support as Clinton's deputy were important. Clinton spoke briefly, acknowledging the trauma and loss that the Haitian people were experiencing, and called for immediate assistance in the rescue and relief efforts followed by a massive reconstruction program. Paul describes Clinton as "pained but confident,"[13] and found his remarks respectful of the Haitians and personally comforting: "On January 13, Clinton's mix of idealism and pragmatism buoyed me up."[14] But Paul is a doctor first and foremost, and he admits he "felt out of place on the UN dais"[15] and just wanted to get to Haiti as soon as possible. By the end of the day, with Secretary Clinton's help, Paul boarded a small private jet headed for Haiti. Also on the plane were two orthopedic surgeons and other doctors with experience treating the critically injured. Paul made it clear that he would be traveling as a private citizen, not as a UN diplomat and would forgo any security or protocols that he knew would slow him down, as he was anxious to get to the General Hospital. After circling the city for an hour, the plane landed around ten o'clock at night, and the group deplaned into complete darkness. Paul describes the scene upon his arrival.

> I have lost track of the times I've flown into Haiti, sometimes during political violence and sometimes during disasters natural and unnatural. But I'd never arrived with a heavier heart than on that day. As soon as we opened the door, it hit us: a charnel-house stench filled the air of the windswept runway. I knew this smell but never imagined I would encounter it in an open space. Now it hung over

the city like a filthy, clinging garment—the stench of a
battlefield without the violent din of war.[16]

Loune Viaud, the director of Zanmi Lasante, PIH's sister
organization in Haiti, and Nancy Dorsinville, one of the
OSE team members, met Paul at the airport. Paul wanted
to go directly to the General Hospital with a stop at a makeshift field hospital near the UN base to consult with PIH
doctors David Walton, Joia Mukherjee, and Louise Ivers.
Louise had been in Haiti during the earthquake, and David
and Joia had flown into the Dominican Republic and come
into Haiti by car earlier in the day. Paul was relieved to see
them and listened carefully to Louise's account of the harrowing events of the past thirty hours. A wall had collapsed
on her car when she was en route to the UN logistics base,
and upon arrival she had found herself the only doctor surrounded by people in desperate straits, many with crushed
limbs. In this situation, she was forced to perform surgery
without anesthesia, pain meds, or antibiotics. Not to do so
would have left patients to die of gangrene.[17]

Unfortunately, as Paul was soon to find out when he arrived at the General Hospital, this terrible situation, where
doctors without access to the tools of their trade had to
resort to desperate measures like operating without anesthesia, was not an isolated incident. On a good day, the
General Hospital in Port-au-Prince is a struggling public
facility—underfunded, with too many patients and too few
staff. However, the hospital's medical director, Dr. Alix
Lassègue, and its chief of nursing, Marlaine Thompson, were
dedicated and excellent professionals, still at work late at
night when Paul arrived. They greeted him warmly, glad to
see him, knowing that Paul would offer moral support and
pragmatic assistance. The hospital complex was in complete

chaos. The courtyard was filled with patients who were afraid to go back into the building because of the frequent aftershocks. There was no electricity, and medical supplies and food were running low. While many dedicated doctors and nurses had reported to work at the General Hospital, they were in shock and, like everyone else in the city, reeling from the trauma of the last two days. As many people with bodies crushed and limbs broken from being trapped in falling buildings streamed into the hospital, what was desperately needed—and not available—were surgeons, operating rooms, and clinicians trained in critical emergency care.

Paul was devastated. Heartbroken by the suffering he saw at the makeshift medical tent where the PIH doctors labored, and the unfolding devastation at the General Hospital, he knew what lay ahead for the tens of thousands of Haitians whose already difficult lives would be further strained by loss of loved ones, serious injury, and now full-on trauma. Paul is good in emergencies, and he remained calm and focused, but those first days were stupefying.

Paul spent his days seeing patients and triaging the worst cases to other sites, including the PIH hospital in Cange and the USNS *Comfort*, a floating hospital with twelve operating rooms that arrived about a week after the quake. Late one night during the first week, he wanted to stay overnight at the hospital, but his coworkers convinced him to get some rest or he would be useless the next day. He made his way to where he was staying, at the home of a good friend. But he was pretty traumatized too, and rest eluded him: "I couldn't sleep. In the dim reaches of misery, insomnia is the constant companion, especially when twenty-first-century people die of nineteenth-century afflictions. . . . I was pursued by the sights and smells and sounds of the day: the unrelieved pain; patients and doctors sprinting outside during an aftershock; the young man in respiratory distress . . . and pervading all, the charnel-house odor from the morgue and under the rubble. . . . Counting sheep kept turning into the grim process of counting the dead."[18] Paul finally fell into a deep sleep around dawn and didn't even feel the aftershock that sent everyone else in the house running outside.

The Grim Lists

It was hard to take in and keep track of all the terrible news that was pouring in from various quarters. As Paul put it, "Thus began, well before the end of day two, the making of grim lists."[19] The National Palace was destroyed. The school of nursing, located next to the General Hospital, was flattened to the ground, and all the nursing students inside dead. Twenty-nine of the public buildings housing the government's various ministries were destroyed, injuring or killing hundreds of Haitian civil servants. The seminary collapsed, and all the young men studying for the priesthood died. The UN headquarters came down, and all 110 UN staff, including our closest colleagues, Mr. Annabi and Mr. da Costa, died in a matter of minutes. One member of the OSE team who happened to be on assignment in Haiti was spared. His name was John; he asked that his last name be omitted from this story. He had stepped outside to call his wife in Belgium because he could not get a phone signal inside the building, and as he stood outside, he watched in horror as the building pancaked down. Moments later, he sent a text that read, "SOS, SOS. We are digging people out with our bare hands." We lost communication with him for several days and then found out that a good friend had asked him to walk with him to his house to check on his family. When they arrived, they found the house in ruins, and his friend's wife and two young sons dead. John left Haiti shortly after, traumatized and suffering from terrible survivor's guilt. Paul and Didi were grateful that their immediate family members were safe, but each day more names were added to the grim list of friends and acquaintances who had lost their lives, within a few weeks reaching almost fifty.

It is impossible to describe the chaos that reigned throughout Port-au-Prince in the days following the earthquake or the scale of the trauma and human suffering. Thousands of people were still trapped in fallen buildings, and rescue workers pushed themselves around the clock to find and free people, many with crushed limbs requiring medical attention that was not available. There were food and water shortages, electricity was out, many roads were impassable, and gas was hard to find. Hundreds of thousands of now homeless people were trying to find a place to live. They had no shelter, no clothing, no food, and no access to bathrooms or showers, and the lack of sanitation soon created unsafe health conditions. The reign of chaos would continue for weeks to come; sadly, for many, it would continue for several years, especially for the million-plus people who had lost their homes and found themselves living, for up to two years, in makeshift tent camps with only a tarp or cardboard roof for protection.

In her book *Lamentations and the Tears of the World,* Kathleen O'Connor engages in an extended discussion of theodicy that I shared with Paul as he grappled with the trauma and suffering in the post-earthquake time. O'Connor lays bare some very difficult and painful propositions about suffering wrought by trauma, destruction, desolation, and the mysterious ways God's absence and presence are experienced in our wounded and broken world. She roundly rejects what I like to call "Have a Nice Day" theology, in which the fears and suffering of the human condition are hidden or dismissed at all costs lest acknowledging them bring us beyond the brink of despair. She demands that Christians recognize that there truly is such a thing as a "house for sorrow, neither denied nor overcome with sentimental wishes, theological escapism, or premature closure."[20]

Haiti was, indeed, a "house for sorrow." Yet the human spirit is strong, and grace always abounds. As Paul testified at the US Senate Committee on Relations two weeks after the earthquake: "Of course not all our colleagues survived. But the vast majority of them did survive, and they have spent the last two weeks working day and night to relieve the staggering suffering of the wounded and displaced. Everywhere we have seen acts of great bravery and solidarity."[21] Scores of physicians and rescue workers from around the world put their busy lives on hold to go and help the Haitians. Over 50 percent of US households donated to Haiti relief. O'Connor suggests that the best—and maybe the only—way to accompany those who are suffering is by showing them "reverent attention" and "companionship."[22] And these two spiritual practices were evident, at both the personal and the institutional levels, in so many different and beautiful ways. By the fourth day, rescue and relief workers and supplies were pouring into Port-au-Prince.

Back in the United States, staff and volunteers at Partners In Health, in Clinton's office, and in the UN Office of the Special Envoy were working around the clock to meet the requests for supplies that were pouring in. Some of the OSE staff were sleeping in the office, catching a few hours of rest when they could. Generous friends lent us their private planes to deliver the supplies and send personnel to Haiti. People we were close to in Haiti were asking for personal items such as clothes, a coffeepot, over-the-counter meds,

soap, shampoo, toothbrushes and toothpaste, and deodor-
ant. Paul and others making frequent trips to Haiti carried
these items, and we often slipped in some candy or little
toys as treats for the children. Paul needed cash too, the only
currency that worked in postdisaster Haiti, so we cobbled
together ten thousand dollars from family and friends and
the generous contribution of a longtime friend of Paul's
whom he calls a "well-respected nun in Miami" in *Haiti
after the Earthquake*.[23]

Clinton made his first visit after the earthquake on day
six. He waited a few extra days as he was concerned about
interrupting rescue and relief efforts with the protocols that
are necessary for a visit from a former US president. Paul
had asked Clinton to include a visit to the General Hospital
and had sent him a long shopping list that included medicines
they could not find in Haiti and dozens of generators.[24] Clinton arrived on the morning of January 18, and Paul went
with Prime Minister Bellerive to meet him. Unfortunately,
there was a mix-up in communication, and they went to the
wrong place and missed the motorcade. Paul was very upset
that he was not standing on the tarmac to greet WJC and
his team. Even the prime minister couldn't get a clear answer
about when the plane landed. The noise at the airport was
deafening, but someone finally shouted at them and let them
know they had missed them and that they were on the way
to the General Hospital. Paul and the prime minister jumped
in his car and tried to catch up with the UN motorcade.
Prime Minister Bellerive consoled Paul, telling him that Clinton was not the kind of person who would take offense
because they were not on hand to greet him, especially in a
disaster zone where the control tower isn't functioning and
phone service is nil. Paul thought, "Exactly right. Clinton
wasn't at all that sort of person; he would already be focused

on rescue and relief. He was also likely to be thinking, already, about reconstruction."[25] They found Clinton at the hospital visiting with patients and staff. There was a mob scene, as so many patients and their families wanted Clinton's attention. Clinton took his time with the patients and their families and then answered questions from a group of journalists with camera crews. One reporter asked the question that Paul himself was planning to ask the former president: "Have you, in your experience, ever seen anything as bad as this?" Clinton paused and then said, "I have seen many large natural disasters, in my country and in others. But never has there been one so concentrated in such a heavily populated part of a densely populated country, one that has devastated a capital city and with this much loss of life and infrastructure." Without pause, he added, "This is worse than what has happened before, but I am confident that Haiti will recover and will build back better."[26]

Paul left that evening on Clinton's plane for a few days in Miami. When he and Bill Clinton were alone on the plane, he asked the question that had haunted him all day. "Why are you confident that Haiti could recover?" The President told him, "Haitians have fought adversity for centuries. There is so much talent here, and perhaps they can turn this reversal into some new opportunities. And think about Rwanda." Clinton's confident words reassured Paul in the following days as he tried to find his way forward.

Two days later, Paul was back in Haiti. He had planned to stay in Miami a little longer to organize some relief efforts and finish an editorial on the earthquake for the *Miami Herald*. But he was restless; he couldn't get his patients off his mind and felt compelled to go back to try to save as many lives as possible and to support and help his colleagues. So he and Louise Ivers sat in my car at a private airstrip, finished the *Herald* editorial, and then, dragging six big duffle bags filled with supplies, caught a ride on a small plane with some doctors from the University of Miami.

Paul reluctantly returned to his duties as Deputy Special Envoy when he was asked to make a trip to Montréal on January 25 for a high-level ministerial meeting to prepare for the upcoming UN donor conference scheduled for March 25 in New York. Paul had mixed feelings about leaving Haiti. Working with patients seemed more attractive to him than sitting around a table talking at an international meeting. However, he wisely realized that "medical care was not going to rebuild Haiti,"[27] so he joined the prime minister and other government officials on the trip to Montréal. Representatives from wealthy nations, multilateral development banks, UN agencies, and other big international players gathered around the table to talk about the future of Haiti. The purpose of the meeting was to discuss the plan and the funds needed for the massive reconstruction effort that would need to be mounted in the coming years. Paul was relieved to hear that all agreed that the Haitian government needed to take the lead, although he knew from experience that concerns would eventually arise about the ability of the Haitians to deliver. He was concerned too that the voices of the Haitian poor would not be heard, so upon returning to his UN office, he came up with a plan to gather testimony from the poor throughout Haiti. Calling the project "The Voice of the Voiceless," he asked Michèle Montas, a Haitian journalist and defender of the rights of the poor who was currently serving as spokesperson for Ban Ki-moon, to head it up. Montas sent Haitian interviewers armed with tape recorders throughout Haiti to gather input from the people whose voices are usually left out of the discussion about their own future. This was to make sure that their views would be included in the data being collected for the Post-Disaster Needs Assessment that would guide the reconstruction plan.

The donor conference, so long in the planning, was held at the General Assembly building of the United Nations on March 25, 2010. Heads of state and many dignitaries were flying in from all over the world, and security was tight. Paul's job was to sit behind Clinton and brief him as needed on the "civil society" session he was chairing. The pledging sessions were in the afternoon. Country by country, governments announced their pledges to help Haiti "build back better," and the total pledged was an extraordinary $9.9 billion. However, our office had been quietly tracking donor pledges during the relief phase, and while it is hard to believe, given the huge amount of money that is pledged at these donor conferences, there was no tracking mechanism in place to monitor whether pledge payments were made and reached the intended recipient. A sharp young Australian woman in our office, Katherine Gilbert, on loan from UNICEF, had developed significant expertise in this area. The information gleaned from her efforts surprised everyone, for it revealed that many pledges were never fulfilled, and when they were, very little of the money was going to the Haitian government. Clinton and Paul agreed that this was terribly wrong: how could the government of Haiti run the country without resources to build infrastructure? Our office continued our tracking project to see how much of the $9.9 billion in pledges was delivered and where the funds were going; the results were dismaying. As of December 2011, only 52.9 percent of the $2.3 billion pledged for the years 2010 and 2011 had arrived. The $1.15 billion the United States had pledged for reconstruction stalled because of partisan politics in Congress. We discovered that some of the funds pledged were actually "repurposed" dollars that had previously been committed elsewhere.[28] And, as usual, very little of the pledged funds went directly to the Haitian government, instead going to NGOs working in Haiti or US contractors. Clinton did not hesitate to call each and every donor nation that had not yet delivered the money they pledged for Haiti, and both the former president and Paul strongly advocated for more direct government support.

The months after the earthquake were a blur for Paul, as they were for so many who were working in the disaster zone. Bone-deep mental and physical fatigue from working seven days a week for eighteen grueling hours a day in the humid heat, often with only one quick meal a day, was taking its toll. There was little time to reflect on all that had occurred, mourn the cumulative losses, or think through important decisions. Paul was constantly scrambling to handle all kinds of crises—medical, administrative, and peacekeeping—as tempers wore thin. Prone to anxiety under normal circumstances, Paul was deeply affected by these distressing times. Making the occasional trip to Cange helped; he would spend the night in his little home there and see his oldest friends, including the elderly Fr. Fritz Lafontant and Mamito, whom he thought of as surrogate parents. They helped to soothe and center him, as did a quiet time sitting by one of his fishponds. And seeing the earthquake victims being treated in a good facility in the PIH hospital in Cange gave him deep satisfaction. He missed Didi and his children terribly. But Didi was grateful that Paul was working in her country, and she was actively fundraising for Haiti in Rwanda and Paris. Anxious as she was to return to Haiti, Paul and Didi agreed that it was not yet safe for the family to travel to Haiti for a visit. In the early spring of 2010, Paul was filled with joy as he made the long trip home to Rwanda for a much-needed family reunion.

Haiti in the Time of Cholera

In mid-October, nine months after the earthquake, Paul was in Rwanda when he got a message from Louise Ivers in Haiti reporting that many patients were arriving in Mirebalais and Saint-Marc with acute, watery diarrhea. Hearing this, Paul says he remembers thinking, "Let's hope it's typhoid."[29] But he doubted it. What seemed most likely was what he most feared: an outbreak of cholera, a deadly disease "known to mow through refugee camps and slums lacking clean water and sanitation, especially after wars and disasters natural and unnatural."[30] Paul was distraught but not surprised.

People who live in wealthy countries with access to decent water and sanitation, even if they themselves are not wealthy, will not get cholera, much less die from it. But Haiti did not have decent municipal water and sanitation systems, so cholera, which is highly contagious, hit Haiti like a bomb, spreading quickly from town to town and then into villages far from any clean or filtered source. The treatment for cholera is massive rehydration to replace the fluids and electrolytes that are rapidly lost through explosive, watery diarrhea. As cholera is caused by a bacterium, antibiotics are also used. Quick treatment is critical, as rapid loss of body fluids leads to severe dehydration and shock, a life-threatening condition. Soon, cases were reported across the country. By the end of 2010, almost two hundred thousand cases had been reported and thousands of people had died.[31] Desperately ill people were coming in droves to hospitals and clinics that were unprepared for the onslaught. The cholera outbreak quickly turned into a full-blown epidemic and a clinical and political nightmare. For the next few months, most of Paul's time and energy were taken up dealing with this new disaster. PIH and other local health care providers moved quickly to set up cholera treatment centers, and they were soon joined by some international health care organizations. Nevertheless, their set-up pace could not keep up with the rapidly spreading disease, and many thousands of lives were lost due to lack of access to treatment.

There were many meetings and long calls with experts in the field to discuss how to respond to and contain the cholera outbreak. Paul anticipated that expert opinion on cholera would be divided, and he was correct: arguments started right away. One camp argued for the primacy of prevention, the other camp for treatment. Some organizations working in the trenches, including Partners In Health, argued for an approach that integrates prevention and treatment, for based on their experience, they believed that a combination of prevention and treatment leads to better outcomes for patients. Such disagreements can become contentious and lead to competition rather than cooperation, which Paul finds deeply discouraging. Still, he always stays the course and fights for what he knows is best for the patients. One major controversy centered around whether to use the cholera vaccine in Haiti. Paul strongly advocated for it, and as the experts argued about it, PIH just went ahead and raised its own funds and piloted its own vaccination campaign.[32]

All hell broke loose when a few months after the epidemic began, it was discovered that cholera had likely been introduced in Haiti by UN peacekeepers from Nepal, whose capital had recently suffered a cholera outbreak. Unbeknownst to them, they were carriers of the disease with no symptoms. The camp where they were living had faulty plumbing with leaky sewage pipes and overflowing holding tanks that were located on the banks of a tributary of the longest river in the country, the two-hundred-mile Artibonite. Raw sewage poured into the river, contaminating the water that people use for drinking and bathing. Those using the water were soon infected with cholera and the disease

then spread rapidly. As charged accusations and counterac-
cusations flew back and forth from all quarters, Paul suggested that a genetic and epidemiological study be done to
identify the particular strain of cholera present in Haiti.
Both the clinical and circumstantial evidence led to the same
conclusion: presumably accidentally, Nepalese peacekeepers
introduced cholera to Haiti. Initially, and for some six years,
the UN denied its culpability. Only in 2016 did the UN
acknowledge its responsibility for bringing cholera to Haiti;
the organization has now apologized to the Haitians and
expressed its desire to make amends.

As 2010 came to a close, the cholera epidemic continued
to ravage Haiti. Paul and his family gathered in Rwanda for
the Christmas holidays in good spirits, happy to be together.
But Paul continued to brood about cholera over the holidays
until finally his teenage daughter asked him to please stop
talking about cholera every night at dinner. He was concerned with good reason: as of the time of this writing,
spring of 2018, the cholera epidemic continues throughout
Haiti, with cases peaking every rainy season.

Blessed Friends at Zanmi Beni

Much of this chapter has been devoted to a story of trauma,
pain, disruption, and suffering, but I close with a story of
hope and friendship, albeit one born out of great tragedy.

Paul turned fifty on October 26, 2009. His family and
several hundred friends gathered in New York to mark this
happy occasion with a birthday party. His college pal, the
well-known peace activist Fr. John Dear, SJ, came from New
Mexico to celebrate Mass at the venerable Jesuit church St.
Ignatius Loyola on Park Avenue. After the Mass, the group
went downstairs to the parish hall for a festive party. In lieu
of gifts, Paul asked for donations to Partners In Health. In

January, a few weeks after the earthquake, he decided how to use some of his birthday money.

When Paul arrived at the General Hospital with Loune Viaud and Nancy Dorsinville thirty hours after the earthquake, Loune and Nancy immediately went to check on a group of children who were living in a dilapidated section of the hospital in a ward with the sad name of "The Abandoned Babies Unit." There were about thirty-six children, many of whom had some type of disability and had been left at the hospital by parents who were sadly unable to care for them. Others were orphaned or had been abused. Pre-earthquake living conditions for the children had been less than optimal, but when the quake hit, the building suffered severe damage and the already-overtaxed hospital staff, overwhelmed with throngs of severely injured people, were unable to provide even basic care for the children. When Paul, Loune, and Nancy arrived at the General Hospital, they found the children alone, hungry, frightened, and surrounded by chaos, injury, disease, and death. It was apparent that something had to be done immediately to protect these children.

All three well understood the challenges they would face in making a long-term commitment to these vulnerable children. However, Paul and Loune could not turn their backs on the children's plight and set out, in a very difficult post-earthquake environment, to receive them as family and establish a long-term, residential home where they would be safe and loved and would have the opportunity to grow and develop to their full potential.

Loune quickly moved all the children to a temporary location in an undamaged hospital run by a physician-priest. It seemed almost miraculous when, in the midst of the devastation of the earthquake, they found a beautiful, sprawling property for sale just outside Port-au-Prince. Paul used his birthday money to purchase the property. Partners In

Health and Zanmi Lasante then formed a partnership with "Papa" Bill Horan at Operation Blessing, and together these three international organizations moved quickly and decisively to develop a plan to convert the property into an appropriate living environment with the necessary accommodations for the children with disabilities. The name chosen for the community was Zanmi Beni, which means "Blessed Friends" in Haitian Creole. In the following year, other children whose parents had died in the earthquake joined the original group, bringing the total number of children in the Zanmi Beni community to sixty-four. Loune, matriarch of the community, lives among the children; in time, she personally adopted all sixty-four children, creating a big family who all share the same last name of Beni. Though born out of terrible tragedy, Zanmi Beni is a beautiful place. Paul calls it a "veritable oasis: a house full of kids . . . surrounded by a few acres of well-tended land, lush with mangoes and other fruit trees."[33]

In December of 2014, twelve Dominican friars joined with over fifty friends of Zanmi Beni and traveled from the United States to Haiti to join the local community in celebrating the baptisms of the Zanmi Beni children. It was a glorious day. The sixty-plus children, thanks to the generosity of a Miami friend, Irene Souto, were dressed in beautiful white outfits. Music filled the air; the Gospel was preached in Creole and English, and there was not a dry eye as the holy water was poured on each precious child. As the children were anointed with an indelible seal uniting them to the heart of Jesus forever, the Christian community welcomed them into the Body of Christ. Many people present commented that it was the closest they had ever been to the kingdom of God on earth.

It was a special day for Paul too as he stood with Didi and their three children on the holy ground of Zanmi Beni, purchased with the money from his birthday. At the baptismal ceremony, Paul spoke to the group:

> Thank you, Padre Eduardo. Thanks to all the Dominicans for such an unforgettable and moving ceremony. It has been a great privilege to be here on this day. I will never forget it.
>
> Friendship is like baptism. It can be an act of faith and demands acts of faith; real friendship does and leaves an indelible mark on the believer.
>
> We are a web of family and friends, and the purpose of these webs is, yes, to instruct but also to protect each other, to look out for each other, to care for each other, especially in difficult times. And there have been many difficult times. Indeed, we were flung together as individuals, and as institutions and across generations, by the events of January 2010—five years ago. And that event and many others . . . they are reminders of why these ties have to be indelible and why they need to be sacramental as well.
>
> It is a simple and blessed enough jump from partner to friend. And then comes the biggest jump of all, the jump from friend to family—[to] caring about each other as much as we would our own children, our own family. This could not be more implicitly the order of Jesus in the gospels; it is as clear as it could be. And it is not an easy thing to do. It requires the process of acknowledging the other, someone who is not related to you, or maybe you don't even know. This is why the Good Samaritan parable is so powerful, because it asks the simple question: "Who is my neighbor?" And the answer was a complete stranger in need.[34]

CHAPTER SIX

Who Lives? Who Dies?

Access to Health Care as a Human Right

Just then a lawyer stood up to test Jesus. "Teacher," he said, "what must I do to inherit eternal life?" He said to him, "What is written in the law? What do you read there?" He answered, "You shall love the Lord your God with all your heart, and with all your soul, and with all your strength, and with all your mind; and your neighbor as yourself." And he said to him, "You have given the right answer; do this, and you will live." . . . [Jesus asked,] "Which of these three, do you think, was a neighbor to the man who fell into the hands of the robbers?" [The expert in the law replied,] "The one who showed him mercy." Jesus said to him, "Go and do likewise."

Luke 10:25-28, 36-37

What is it like to feel the earth tremble and see the roof and walls of your home or school fall towards you? More to the point, in terms of survival: what happens next? It depends. Not just on the severity of the injury, but on who and where you are. Who lives and who dies depends on what sort of health-care system is available. And who recovers, if recovery is possible, depends on the way emergency care and hospitals are financed.[1]

Paul Farmer

A Year of Incalculable Loss

The year following the January earthquake was a season of loss for Paul. He had lost over fifty friends and coworkers in the earthquake with little time to mourn. There were many memorial services in New York for some of the 110 UN colleagues who died when the UN headquarters in Haiti came tumbling down. In June, the matriarch of Cange, Mamito Lafontant, died from a stroke. She and her husband, Fr. Fritz, had given Paul his start during his first year in Haiti, and he had remained very close to them. Paul describes how she influenced him in this way: "Mamito had taught me a lot over the previous twenty-seven years. She liked to give instructions, but her version of 'wipe your feet' or 'clean your room' were broader in scope, if equally to the point: 'Make this house waterproof for this family; put tin on the roof and cement the floor.' She issued more maternal fiats as well, and everyone who visited Cange got a little dose of Mamito's mothering."[2] Mamito worked until the very end of her life; her last days were spent on earthquake relief work, helping the many volunteer doctors and nurses who came to work at the hospital in Cange, which was filled with earthquake victims. Didi came from Rwanda for Mamito's funeral, for Mamito had been a mother to her too. Her passing left a huge void in Paul and Didi's lives.

In early September, Paul was in Rwanda preparing to head to Haiti to meet Clinton to mark the occasion of the first anniversary of the earthquake when Ophelia Dahl called to tell him that Tom White had died. Tom was ninety and, as was his plan, had died a poor man after having given away his entire fortune—so much so that in his last years, when Ophelia asked for financial assistance for a PIH project, he told her didn't have any money left but that she could use his house as collateral to get a bank loan. Paul was honored when Tom's widow, Lois, asked him to give the eulogy at Tom's funeral. For Paul, the death of Tom and the first anniversary of the earthquake were "all jumbled together."[3]

When Paul is sad or upset, he becomes quiet. His usually outgoing personality shuts down a bit, and he becomes pensive, lost in his thoughts, sometimes looking down while biting on his lip or thumb. He might ask a theological or philosophical question to try to understand or give meaning to what is on his mind, but mostly he is quiet, and if circumstances allow, he will likely retreat and go off alone. As the first anniversary of the earthquake approached and he took in the loss of his great friend and partner, he was *very* quiet and very much in need of some time alone. In the days between Tom's death and his funeral, Paul kept slipping away for hours at a time to mourn, to pray, and to reflect on Tom's life and largesse. In these quiet hours, he wrote a beautiful and moving tribute to Tom, delivered on January 11, 2011, in the Church of Saint Ignatius of Loyola on the grounds of Boston College. The church was packed, filled with friends from the world over, many of them beneficiaries of Tom's decades of generosity, to pay tribute and to honor Tom's life and legacy. Paul's words about Tom, spoken emotionally and with much love, captured the essence of a holy man who loved his fellow humans:

Tom knew his math but also taught many of us (to borrow from Ephesians) that we sometimes see best with the eyes of the heart. He did not, in his charitable work, take short cuts or avoid the hard process of discernment. Tom knew that everyone in this world can and does suffer, but he also knew that some suffer more than others and that many suffer injustice.

Tom's generosity did not require proximity. His imagination, and the eyes of his heart, allowed him to understand suffering unlike any he had seen, even in the theatre of war. That's why his generosity was legendary not just in his hometown but around the world.[4]

After laying his beloved friend to rest, Paul had to head directly to Port-au-Prince, as the first anniversary of the earthquake was the very next day. It was a long, hard day for Paul. Port-au-Prince still looked the same as it did a year earlier: it would take a couple of years to remove the rubble from all the collapsed buildings. Over one million people were living in makeshift tent camps in what can only be described as inhumane living conditions. Paul accompanied the "indefatigable"[5] Clinton to two commemorative events and a visit to the General Hospital. Like the rest of the city, it looked just as it had a year earlier, the only addition being a new tent housing a cholera treatment unit. Nevertheless, the dedicated staff who greeted them were still working as hard as ever. The cholera epidemic had not abated, and the national plan for the cholera response was still stalled while the experts continued to debate what the plan should include. Port-au-Prince was somber, with prayer services and solemn ceremonies taking place around the city. At one event, Prime Minister Bellerive remembered the 316,000[6] people who died in the earthquake. By the end of the day,

Paul was spent. He admits his exhaustion and sadness: "For those of a less formidable constitution, it was time for solitary reflection. Not feeling very prayerful, I retreated to Maryse's house to contemplate the year quietly and alone."[7]

In the midst of this season of loss, with an eye to the upcoming challenge of reconstruction, Paul made the time to write a book about the harrowing events in the year following the January 2010 earthquake. His friends and colleagues encouraged this project, believing that Paul, given his deep knowledge of Haiti, his twenty-five years of on-the-ground experience, and his perspectives gained from his different roles—physician, academic, service provider, and UN diplomat—was best placed to record for posterity what occurred in post-earthquake Haiti. Paul wrote two thirds of the book, entitled *Haiti after the Earthquake,* and invited twelve of his Haitian and American colleagues to write chapters sharing their own experiences and perspectives. The combination of Paul's comprehensive overview with these diverse voices makes for an informative and compelling read. The book, published in July of 2011, is dedicated to his dear friends Al and Diane Kaneb, two of the kindest, most encouraging, most generous people in Paul's life, fellow Catholics who share Paul's love for the poor and commitment to the corporal works of mercy. In many instances over the years, Diane and Al's generous financial support has kept Partners In Health afloat.

In the midst of the earthquake year, an important book that had been a couple of years in the making was released. Called *Partner to the Poor: A Paul Farmer Reader*, the book is an edited compilation of a wide variety of Paul's writings over the previous two decades. The thick volume is expertly edited by Haun Saussy, whom Paul likes to refer to as "the most brilliant man in the world." Haun and Paul have been friends since they were undergraduates at Duke, and Paul's assessment of Haun's intellect is pretty accurate; he is a university professor at the University of Chicago and a widely published, erudite scholar in the field of comparative literature. But what really sets Haun apart is his gentle nature, good humor, and generous ways. Paul often turns to Haun for editing advice, and his skills and speed are unmatched, as is his willingness to set aside his own work to assist.

Reconstruction and the Mirebalais Hospital

Perhaps Paul's greatest source of consolation and hope in this season of loss was Partners In Health's ambitious reconstruction project: a three-hundred-bed, state-of-the-art teaching hospital in Mirebalais, just a few miles from where Paul had worked as a young man during his first year in Haiti. Prior to the earthquake, PIH had been planning to build a small community hospital in Mirebalais, but at the request of Alex Larsen, the Haitian minister of health, they made the bold decision to dramatically increase the size and scope of the project in the aftermath of the quake by building a world-class teaching hospital. "Why not try something really bold and beautiful?" Paul asked. Not everyone agreed with this decision, and some even tried to talk Paul out of going forward with the plan; the detractors thought it was fine to be ambitious but that this project, three times bigger than anything they had ever attempted, was *too* ambitious and too risky. But Paul would have none of it and forged ahead with the project. Another college friend from Duke, Ann Clark, now an architect in Chicago, was the principal designer, donating the services of her firm. One of Paul's protégés, Dr. David Walton, headed up the team that would bring this complex project to fruition. A successful Boston contractor, Jim Ansara, volunteered his time and significant resources overseeing the construction of the hospital and ensured adherence to the highest building standards and the use of the best-quality materials.

The hospital cost $17 million to build, a fraction of what it would cost to build a three-hundred-bed teaching hospital in the United States. It took three years of blood, sweat, and tears to build the hospital, but the result is spectacular. The buildings and grounds are beautiful. Gardens and courtyards are an integral part of the design to encourage natural ventilation for cooling as well as to prevent the transmission of tuberculosis and other airborne diseases. Large shading roofs protect the interior from the hot tropical sun, and natural daylighting is used to conserve energy for hospital equipment. The entire complex is solar powered, and high-efficiency ceiling fans and lighting further reduce energy usage. The main medical campus has seven buildings, six operating rooms, laboratories, radiology, a neonatal unit, a rehab center, and the only CT scanner in Haiti available to the poor without fees, donated by Paul's good friends Stephen and Pilar Crespi Robert. When touring the hospital as it was opening, Stephen and Pilar asked Paul what was going to fill an empty room they had just passed. Paul told them, "Someday we hope to get a CT scanner—it is hard to be a world-class hospital without one." They glanced at each other and said without hesitation, "Please let us get it for you." On a visit the following year to see the CT scanner in action, Stephen and Pilar asked about the plans for a vacant lot on the property adjacent to the hospital. Paul told them that someday he hoped to build a world-class laboratory for the hospital. Again, they glanced at each other, and on that lot now stands a state-of-the-art lab. There are many other stories like this one about dozens of generous friends, corporations, and supporters who partnered with PIH to raise the funds to design, build, and outfit the hospital and who continue to help with operating funds because they believe that good health care should be available to people everywhere, especially to people living on the margin of extreme poverty.[8]

The hospital, which is owned by the Haitian government and operated by Partners In Health/Zanmi Lasante, provides primary care services to about 185,000 people in Mirebalais and two nearby communities. But patients from a much wider area—all of central Haiti and areas in and around Port-au-Prince—also receive secondary and tertiary care there. The hospital sees as many as 700 patients every day in its ambulatory clinics and has become the training ground for the next generation of Haitian medical students, resident physicians, and nurses. Paul decided to call it the Hôpital Universitaire de Mirebalais (University Hospital), HUM for short. Someone once asked Paul, "Why is it called university hospital? There is no university!" With a little smile, Paul responded, "Not yet!" Although many other post-earthquake reconstruction projects struggled and faltered, HUM stands proud as an example of what is possible in post-earthquake Haiti.

The mandate for the United Nations Office of the Special Envoy for Haiti was extended for another year to continue to support post-earthquake Haiti, and now Clinton, Paul, and the team turned the focus of our work to the complex task of assisting with the reconstruction plans.

Bill Clinton's commitment never wavered as he continued to travel to Haiti regularly, sometimes even spending the night in one of the camps. With Prime Minister Bellerive, he cochaired the Interim Haiti Recovery Commission (IHRC), a new entity created to coordinate and oversee the disbursement of reconstruction funds to ensure that the planning efforts and projects were in keeping with the national plan. It was hoped that the IHRC would increase efficiency and transparency and allay the concerns of donor nations. However, the IHRC was a short-term solution, only in existence for eighteen months, certainly not long enough to address the rebuilding of Port-au-Prince in a systematic and comprehensive way. As Paul predicted, there were ongoing concerns about the Haitian government's ability to deliver and tensions raised by some large donors who wanted more control. Other donors wanted to strike out on their own and bypass the commissions, and the Haitians were worried (with good reason) that the funds would go to US contractors and NGOs.[9]

Back in New York, Paul's UN team continued to track the pledges, which were slow to arrive. When they did arrive, very little went to help the Haitian government rebuild their decimated infrastructure. What became clear, which was no surprise to Paul, was that there are many problems with the way foreign aid works. Most of the money that came into Haiti from both governments and philanthropy went to US contractors and nonprofit organizations, some of which had little experience in Haiti and did not plan to stay long-term, and almost nothing went to the Haitian government or Haitian-led organizations. Two data points make this clear. First, less than 1 percent of the $2.4 billion in immediate relief went to the Haitian government. Second, since 2010, USAID has disbursed at least $2.13 billion in contracts and grants for Haiti-related work. Overall, just 2 percent ($48.6 million) went directly to Haitian organizations or firms, compared to more than 56 percent (more than $1.2 billion) to firms located in DC, Maryland, or Virginia.[10] Haiti is often characterized as a black hole for aid, but this designation is patently unfair given that so little funding goes to the

Haitian government or Haitian-led organizations. Nonetheless, the Haitians are often blamed for failures across the board, although they were almost never in charge of the failed projects.

In 2012, after having been extended for a year, the Office of the Special Envoy for Haiti ended its mission, and the office closed. At that time, Clinton approached the UN secretary-general and suggested that he consider appointing Paul as a special adviser to ensure that the lessons learned in Haiti in the recent years would not be lost. Mr. Ban accepted Clinton's suggestion, and Paul was named Special Adviser to the Secretary-General on Community-Based Medicine and Lessons from Haiti. Such prestigious volunteer positions are generally reserved for world leaders and visionaries with expertise on topics of international interest and importance. Paul established a New York office, bringing several members of the OSE team to work with him to continue the advocacy and tracking efforts of the Office of the Special Envoy for Haiti.

A Fateful Visit to West Africa

In March of 2014, the world began to hear the terrifying news of an Ebola outbreak in West Africa. It would become the largest outbreak in history, with 28,652 cases and 11,325 deaths.[11] In June of 2014, Paul and Didi were scheduled to attend a meeting of the Lancet Commission on Global Surgery being held in Freetown, the capital of Sierra Leone, one of the three West African countries, along with Liberia and Guinea, affected by the Ebola outbreak. Some meeting attendees had wanted to move it because of the Ebola outbreak, but Paul argued against moving the meeting. He thought they should keep the meeting there precisely *because* of the Ebola crisis, and he quipped, "Besides, you don't get Ebola from attending a meeting." As the talk at the Freetown meeting turned to the Ebola outbreak, the group visited a local medical facility that Paul could immediately see was unequipped to care for those stricken with Ebola.

The first cases of Ebola had been reported in March, and in the coming months, the World Health Organization (WHO) and the US Centers for Disease Control and Prevention (CDC) began tracking the outbreak and working with *Médecins Sans Frontières* (Doctors Without Borders) to attempt to control the spread and treat Ebola victims. However, it soon became clear that their efforts were not outpacing the problem. As the Ebola crisis unfolded, and Paul received more information about what was occurring in West Africa, he was deeply troubled. On July 29, 2014, Paul received the news that a colleague, Humarr Khan, a Sierra Leonean doctor working on the front lines of the outbreak, had been struck down by Ebola at 39 years old. Paul couldn't get Khan's death off of his mind, and he began to track the clinical situation in West Africa carefully—obsessively, some of his friends might even say.

Ebola is a terrifying disease, the stuff of the book of Job. It is what is known as a zoonosis; it leaps from animal hosts to humans. People with Ebola quickly become desperately ill with fever, vomiting, and diarrhea followed by rapid dehydration. As the disease runs its course, victims can become delirious, and if they have been fortunate enough to receive fluids from intravenous lines, there can be hemorrhaging from the mouth, the nose, the vagina, and even the eyes. Highly contagious, it is spread through exposure to bodily fluids, including blood, urine, sweat, semen, breast milk, vomit, and diarrhea. The virus remains viable and infectious even after the patient has died, and thus preparing the dead for burial can itself become a death sentence. Ebola is, as Paul puts it, "a caregivers' disease,"[12] spread by caring for family members. Ebola can, and often did, infect and kill entire families in a matter of a month. More than 75 percent of Ebola victims were women.

By August, Paul was gripped with a "pervasive anxiety."[13] Upset about Humarr Khan's death, and seeing Ebola on a killing spree as it rapidly spread into a full-blown epidemic, he didn't feel he could just watch from the sidelines any longer. He felt compelled to join the fight against Ebola and went to his colleagues and the Partners In Health board with an impassioned plea to consider going to work in West Africa. The PIH model differs significantly from that of other NGOs such as Doctors Without Borders, which come for the short term to try to stem the spread of the epidemic and care for desperately ill people and then depart when the crisis has passed. In contrast, PIH comes for the long haul, sets down deep roots to make common cause with the local community, and invests in building health care systems. For PIH, a decision to set up shop in West Africa would have serious long-term financial and human resource consequences. And like everyone involved in any way with the Ebola outbreak, PIH staff, their family members, and their advisers were afraid. Only someone crazy would not be. But PIH is courageous and did not let its fears determine its course of action. In September of 2014, Paul and five colleagues headed to West Africa to meet with government officials in Sierra Leone and Liberia to request an assignment. They made a wise decision to partner with two community-based health care delivery organizations already working in the region: Last Mile Health in Liberia and Wellbody Alliance in Sierra Leone.

Partners In Health was under no illusions about the challenges it would face in West Africa. The staff were fully aware that there were no properly equipped hospitals and that they would be operating in situations where they lacked much of what was needed to provide high-quality care to the patients. Because of the way the Ebola virus is transmitted, all medical personnel coming in contact with a patient would have to don cumbersome personal protective equipment (PPE)—a heavy suit, gloves, and a face mask that provide head-to-toe coverage. Using PPE is difficult and slows medical personnel down. They have to work in short shifts because PPE gear can be kept on only for a few hours at a time due to overheating and perspiration within the suits, made worse by lack of air conditioning in sweltering buildings. There is a strict protocol for putting on and removing the equipment, and failure to follow it properly can result in deadly infection. Furthermore, the gear can be used only once and must be burned afterwards. As PIH began to marshal resources to get up and running quickly in Sierra Leone and Liberia, Paul started writing and speaking about the Ebola epidemic in a wide variety of media outlets, academic publications, and speaking engagements in order to aggressively counter both the prevailing narrative about the cause of the epidemic and the notion that Ebola is an automatic death sentence.

Staff, Stuff, Space, and Systems

The titles of Paul's talks and articles usually speak for themselves. In the *Washington Post*, he published "The Secret to Curing West Africa from Ebola Is No Secret at All."[14] In the *Huffington Post*, he claimed that "Ebola Does Not Need to Be a Death Sentence."[15] Other titles include "The Ebola Outbreak, Fragile Health Systems and Quality as a

Cure" (*Journal of the American Medical Association*)[16] and "Who Lives and Who Dies: Paul Farmer on the Iniquities of Healthcare Funding" (*London Review of Books*).[17] In almost every article he wrote and talk he gave, Paul laid out his central claims about why the Ebola epidemic occurred, the steps that needed to be taken to control and end the crisis, what kind of treatment Ebola victims should receive, and what needs to happen so that poor countries don't continually find themselves prey to these devastating crises. Paul's thinking differs significantly from, indeed opposes, many of the prevailing ideas about Ebola propounded by "experts" who often make immodest claims of causality. Paul's position on Ebola is vintage Farmer; in fact, he has clearly stated these arguments in different formats for many years. However, the drama of the unfolding Ebola epidemic presented an opportunity to express these concepts with immediacy and clarity.

His first claim is that it is *weak health systems, not the virus, that are to blame for Ebola's rapid spread and its high case-fatality rates.* Paul and his colleagues point out that "if the Ebola virus surfaced in Boston or Toronto, there is little doubt that their health systems, despite shortcomings, could effectively contain and then eliminate the disease with far lower fatality rates than those in West Africa."[18] In robust medical settings, Ebola can be stopped by linking better infection control (to protect the uninfected) to improved clinical care (to save the afflicted). He argues that pitting prevention against treatment needs to stop, for both have a critical role to play and are equally necessary. While stopping transmission is essential, especially in the absence of an effective medical system, it is not a durable, long-term solution. The long-term solution is to invest in building strong health care systems in poor countries so they have the capacity both to offer good primary care and properly treat patients in a crisis and to respond quickly to control outbreaks when emergency situations arise in the future, which they inevitably will.

His second claim is that *stopping the spread of Ebola and treating it (or for that matter, any disease) are simply not possible without "staff, stuff, space, and systems."* The phrase "staff, stuff, space, and systems" would become Paul's mantra in the coming years as he advocated for "the availability of adequate health care staff, resources, and systems required for the delivery of high-quality health care services."[19]

Staff. In Liberia at the time of the outbreak, there were just 51 doctors, fewer than many clinical units have in a typical US teaching hospital,[20] to serve 4.3 million people, and many of these clinicians died from Ebola, further reducing the already small number of health care workers. Many more physicians are needed, but this is not enough. Nurses trained to deliver supportive care such as electrolyte management and other life-saving measures are needed, along with well-trained community health workers who can encourage patients to seek medical attention early.

Stuff. The standard tools of the trade found in plenty and taken for granted in wealthy and middle-income countries are essential for delivery of high-quality medical care. These include medication, basic supplies like thermometers, bandages, alcohol, beds and furniture, cleaning supplies, internet access and telecommunications, and modern medical equipment. Also essential are infection control resources such as proper protective gowns and gloves, intravenous fluids, and the lines to deliver fluids, all of which were in short supply or nonexistent in Sierra Leone and Liberia (as they are in most poor countries). And of course, a well-functioning supply chain to avoid stockouts of critical supplies is critical.

Space. For medical care to be high quality, it must be delivered in a well-designed, appropriate, and safe location.

During the Ebola outbreak, doctors and nurses were working in makeshift facilities in deplorable, frightening, and dangerous conditions. The buildings, or in some cases, tents, were so overcrowded that patients arriving for treatment often died outside the building entrance, lying in their own vomit and diarrhea, as their family members wept over their bodies. It was no better inside the buildings. There were not enough beds, so patients were lying on the floor, and buildings often did not have running water or electricity, which meant there was no air conditioning. Temperatures in the building would reach one hundred degrees, even higher inside the protective equipment. And no matter how much bleach was dumped on the floors, the buildings were filthy and smelled terrible.

Systems. High-quality medical care cannot be delivered without the careful coordination of a wide range of actions and interventions that develop orderly systems to deliver medical care. These systems must comprehensively address the three main components that measure quality: "care that is safe, care that is effective, and care that is delivered in a way that respects the dignity of the individual."[21]

These two key claims—first, that it is weak health systems, not diseases, that are at fault in poor countries; and second, that it is not possible to build good health care systems without access to "staff, stuff, space, and systems"—sum up Paul's operational philosophy. Critics, often global health experts, are quick to say that Paul's claims are "not realistic, not sustainable, not cost-effective." But this is just not true. Evidence from other PIH hospitals in Rwanda, Peru, and Russia has proved otherwise. Safe, effective, and respectful care is being provided, on a large scale, to millions of patients around the world. The argument that offering high-quality medical care is not "cost-effective" is particularly egregious. First, the data suggest otherwise; the cost of providing quality health care need not be higher than that of providing mediocre or no care at all.[22] Second, what is the cost of inaction? Millions of people dying before their time from treatable diseases. It is a terrible moral failing if this does not weigh on the collective conscience of those who do have access to health care. Finally, by the time the Ebola epidemic came to an end, over 11,000 people had died, and upwards of $3 billion had been spent. The economies of the three countries were deeply affected, and the World Bank estimated that they would lose at least $2.2 billion in economic growth in 2015 as a result of the epidemic, a terrible setback for already-struggling countries. Although the responders who came to help were noble and brave, they left nothing behind, so these struggling countries still have the same weak health care systems that leave their people vulnerable to the next epidemic. This begs the question of whether it would be more effective to create a permanent solution by assisting these countries in building strong and stable health care systems, which could surely be done with a much lower price tag than $3 billion.

By January 2015, four months after the September visit to West Africa, Partners In Health was supporting twenty-one facilities—from hospitals to small heath centers—in such far-flung places like Freetown, the Kono and Port Loko Districts in Sierra Leone, and Maryland and Grand Gedeh Counties in Liberia. PIH had shipped tons of supplies and had trained and deployed about two hundred doctors and nurses and other clinical professionals (many of them selfless volunteers) to provide care to patients. As is their way, PIH hired approximately two thousand locals as support staff, community health workers, and orphan caregivers. Their hires included a big group of Ebola survivors, who often faced community stigma and were unable to find employment.

Once the epidemic was under control, PIH turned to the second, long-term phase of their work: strengthening the health systems in Sierra Leone and Liberia. They had two immediate goals: first, to improve primary health care, which had been almost nonexistent during the Ebola outbreak, by focusing on maternal health and safe births and treating illnesses like malaria and TB; and second, to screen approximately four thousand Ebola survivors in Sierra Leone for post-Ebola complications such as uveitis, an inflammation of the eye that can lead to blindness. PIH continues to work putting systems in place, refurbishing and improving facilities, and training community health workers to reach out and build relationships in the community where so many people are suffering from trauma and loss.

The West Africa Commute

From the beginning of the Ebola epidemic in March of 2014, until the WHO officially declared its end in January of 2016 (although other cases would continue to be reported for some time), Paul commuted back and forth from the United States to West Africa. These years were grueling. During the first year, the Ebola epidemic created a good bit of worldwide hysteria—borders closed and quarantines set in around the world. Every time Paul arrived back in the United States, he had to call in his temperature twice daily for twenty-one days to a quarantine officer at the CDC.

As is his way, Paul developed many significant relationships within the local community. In this case, he befriended a big group of men and women, mostly young, all survivors of the deadly Ebola virus. Over time, as they got to know and gain trust in each other, the survivors began to share their heartbreaking stories of pain, loss, and suffering with

Paul. On his many visits to the devastated region, Paul organizes dinners and parties for the PIH staff and his survivor friends who have lived to tell the harrowing narrative of their Ebola epidemic. These occasions, filled with lively conversation, laughter, and sometimes tears, are a testimony to the human spirit and the power of relationships to heal the brokenhearted. During these years, Paul has steadily worked on a book chronicling the Ebola epidemic. Entitled *Fevers, Feuds and Diamonds*, it is a scholarly and comprehensive work that integrates history, medicine, anthropology, health care policy, and service delivery. In particular, the stories of the lives of several Ebola survivors are beautifully written and very moving.[23]

In 2016, Didi and the children left Rwanda after almost ten productive and fulfilling years and returned to Miami. Paul wanted the family closer, and Didi planned to focus on building the Women and Girls Initiative, a wonderful project empowering young women that she had started in Haiti. Catherine has followed her father to his alma mater, Duke University, and Paul and Didi wanted the two younger children, now in grade school, to be educated in the United States.

The 2014–2016 Ebola epidemic years were extremely challenging on many fronts. There were enormous financial and administrative pressures on PIH as they scaled up their work in Liberia and Sierra Leone, and Paul had to dedicate a lot of time and energy to fundraising. The international travel was demanding, as was in-country travel to the rural places where PIH was working. Paul diligently tried to keep up with his Harvard teaching and administrative duties and to publish extensively on the unfolding nightmare in West Africa in order to influence the world's response. Being in the midst of "vast topographies of pain," in the words of Kathleen O'Connor, took its toll emotionally and physically.

And for two long years, as clinicians labored to control the spread of the deadly disease, there was the constant worry about physical safety.

As it happened, Paul's departure for his first trip to work in West Africa fell on the Vigil of the Feast of Our Lady of Sorrows, to whom he has a great devotion. While Paul's family and close friends had again promised their unfailing support, they were worried about his safety. Paul had spent the better part of the last thirty years in some pretty dangerous places and had been exposed to multiple infectious diseases many times over—and on more than one occasion had contracted one himself—but his family and friends thought this time was different, more dangerous than in the past. They knew how much chaos and fear there were in the local communities, with desperately ill people at death's door showing up at Ebola treatment centers that were understaffed and had no orderly treatment protocols yet in place. Understanding how the virus is transmitted and the need for protective equipment when treating patients added to the concern of family and friends: they feared, probably with good reason, that if Paul, for example, came upon a child lying on the ground writhing in pain, there was little chance that he would pass by without attending to her, without showing her the mercy demanded in one of his favorite Scripture passages, the Good Samaritan. In the days leading up to his departure, there were many calls and much begging for prudence and good judgment. On the evening before his departure, we prayed together, calling upon the Risen Lord and Our Lady of Sorrows to accompany Paul as he set out to try to bring about the kingdom of God in the here and now in one of the most ravaged spots in the world.

Thus, on September 14, 2014, we read from the book of Tobit:

[Tobit] called his son and said to him, "Son, prepare supplies for the journey and set out with your brother. May God in heaven bring you safely there and return you in good health to me; and may his angel, my son, accompany you both for your safety. (5:17b)

And then we prayed for Paul:

Gracious God, we ask blessing on your son Paul as he empties himself in love and service to our broken world.

Faithful and loving God, we ask blessings on our brother Paul as he travels to West Africa to be your hands and ears, and mind and heart, and bring the Good News of your love to our suffering brothers and sisters.

Compassionate God, we beg you to protect him and those he travels with;
We beg you to guide him and comfort him as he comforts others;
We beg you to surround him with the peace and light of the Risen Lord;
We beg you to bring him home safely, so he may continue to love and serve you.

Paul, may the Lord guide you in the path of peace, and may He send Our Lady of Sorrows to accompany you on your way, that safe and sound, in peace and joy, you may return to those who love you.

We ask all this through Christ our Lord, who lives and reigns with you and the Holy Spirit, one God forever and ever. Amen.

We are grateful that our prayers were answered.

Accompaniment

Sharing the Gift of Christian Hope

"Blessed are the poor in spirit, for theirs is the
kingdom of heaven.
"Blessed are those who mourn, for they will be
comforted.
"Blessed are the meek, for they will inherit the earth.
"Blessed are those who hunger and thirst for
righteousness, for they will be filled.
"Blessed are the merciful, for they will receive mercy.
"Blessed are the pure in heart, for they will see God.
"Blessed are the peacemakers, for they will be
called children of God.
"Blessed are those who are persecuted for
righteousness' sake, for theirs is the kingdom
of heaven."

Matthew 5:3-10

Accompaniment does not privilege technical expertise
above solidarity or compassion or a willingness to
tackle what may seem to be insuperable challenges.[1]

Paul Farmer

To Walk with Another

This book began with a deliberately provocative claim: "Once in a great while, you meet someone who makes you believe that it is possible to build up the kingdom of God in the here and now. For me and many others, Dr. Paul Farmer is such a person." I hope the narration of Paul's work bringing modern medicine to the poorest people in the world, and his commitment to join the poor in their fight for social and economic rights, gives the reader a good sense of why this is so. However, there is one additional aspect of the Paul Farmer story to include. This piece is what sets Paul apart from many others doing the same good work and is the key to understanding why I think Paul makes it possible to believe that *the kingdom of God* can be built in the *here and now*. Thus, this closing chapter will turn to what I consider the central organizing principle of Paul's life: his wholehearted engagement in the spiritual practice of *accompaniment*. For Paul, accompaniment is an all-encompassing way of life. It guides and colors his every decision and his every action, both professionally and personally, and is the foundation of his moral and spiritual life.

Paul's response to Fr. Gustavo's haunting question of "how [can we] say and . . . show to persons living in the structure of violence, living in social injustice and seeming insignificance, that 'God loves you'?"[2] has been to freely and consciously choose to give himself over to accompanying the world's poorest people on a journey away from suffering and premature death. However, Paul's practice of accompaniment extends beyond just the destitute sick. He notes that the idea of accompaniment "is not diluted by noting that everyone who draws breath needs accompaniment at some stage of life, as long as we acknowledge that some need it more than others."[3] Accompaniment is the cornerstone of his personal and professional life, and it is the primary way he understands his relationality with others, whether they be colleagues, friends, coworkers, students, donors, or government officials. Paul often speaks of and writes about the "accompaniment model" and encourages others to adopt an accompaniment mindset in their own lives. Paul also shares, with honestly and vulnerability, his own need to be accompanied.

The spiritual practice of accompaniment is a deeply personal and highly relational experience. Jean Vanier, founder of the L'Arche communities and another proponent of accompaniment, tells us that "the word 'accompaniment,' like the word 'companion,' comes from the Latin words *cum pane,* which mean 'with bread.' It implies sharing together, eating together, nourishing each other, walking together. The one who accompanies is like a midwife, helping us to come to life to live more fully. But the *accompagnateur* receives life also, and as people open up to each other, a communion of hearts develops between them."[4] Paul agrees with theologian Roberto Goizueta's simple definition of accompaniment: "To accompany another person is to walk with him or her. It is, above all, by walking with others that we relate to them and love them."[5] Goizueta believes that the act of walking with another is "always a fundamentally religious, sacramental act,"[6] and that, like all sacramental acts, accompaniment mediates God's love and mercy. Paul's understanding of accompaniment directly opposes the modern idea of an autonomous self, challenges the narrowness of a life of self-involvement, and calls for an open-ended commitment that he describes in this way:

> Accompaniment is an elastic term: it means just what you'd imagine, and more. To accompany someone is to go somewhere with him or her, to break bread together, to be present on a journey with a beginning and an end. There's

an element of mystery, of openness, in accompaniment. The companion, the *accompagnateur*, says, "I'll go with you and support you on your journey wherever it leads. I'll keep you company and share your fate for a while—and by 'a while,' I don't mean a little while." Accompaniment is about sticking with a task until it's deemed complete— not by the *accompagnateur* but by the person being accompanied.[7]

Accompagnateur as Hope Giver

Early on in their work, PIH realized that if its patients were going to benefit from their medical treatment, they would need assistance managing the terrible hardships in their daily lives created by crushing poverty. It is hard to get better if you are starving or don't have clean water with which to take your meds. PIH saw that their patients needed a wide array of long-term social supports, including food, water, money, transportation, family support, childcare, steady companionship, and psychological counseling. PIH took to calling these complex wraparound services "accompaniment" and found that "when good clinical care— the right diagnosis and treatment plan—is followed by robust accompaniment, we could expect cure rates for tuberculosis to go from around 50 percent to close to 100 percent."[8] Replicating this same model at PIH sites around the world while treating patients with HIV/AIDS and other infectious diseases has yielded the same excellent cure rates.

Accompagnateur, from the French word meaning "to accompany," is a term coined by PIH to describe an individual who accompanies another while he or she is receiving medical treatment. The role of *accompagnateurs* goes beyond medical treatment; they accompany others on an intimate journey that involves what is most personal—family, children, health, sustenance, daily existence—and what is most universal—pain, suffering, fears, and hope. Usually local members of the community, *accompagnateurs* receive extensive training and are paid a stipend for their work, which Partners In Health believes justice requires. Described as a "trusted friend, servant of the community, reliable, credible, responsible, compassionate, and essential for survival, an *accompagnateur* cares about the dignity of the people and solidarity."[9] In his or her presence, constancy, and compassionate outreach, each *accompagnateur* is a hope giver modeling God's love and hospitality.

Over the years, Paul has taken the concept of accompaniment and broadened its meaning and application to include an institutional dimension because he believes governance and public policy can benefit from notions like accompaniment and a preferential option for the poor. In 2011, he delivered the commencement address at Harvard's Kennedy School of Government organized around the theme of accompaniment—its purpose and power. Entitled "Accompaniment as Policy," Paul gave liberation theology, his mentor Fr. Gustavo, and the work of Roberto Goizueta credit for inspiring him and helping him understand accompaniment, and he told the audience how accompaniment has shaped his own life and work. Paul challenged the graduates, most of whom were soon to embark on high-level careers as leaders and policy makers in governance, the NGO world, and private consulting, to incorporate accompaniment principles into their thinking and actions, telling them that "just because we cannot yet measure the value of accompaniment doesn't mean it cannot serve as a guiding principle."[10]

Using hard data and anecdotal evidence from the relief and recovery effort in Haiti after the earthquake, Paul showed how depending on "expertise" alone often leads to failure when implementing policies and plans. Paul explained that using accompaniment principles is "good insurance"[11] against the failures that frequently occur during the implementation phase. Accompaniment demands proximity to the actual physical location where a plan or policy will be implemented and uses different assessment tools to evaluate the needs of the situation and the success of its outcomes. This always includes engaging the local community, listening to those who are going to be directly affected by these decisions, and surveying the local conditions to make sure that what is being planned addresses the reality of the situation. Paul argues that it is "easy to be dismissive of accompaniment in a world in which arcane expertise is advanced as the answer to every problem. But expertise alone will not solve the difficult problems. This was the long, hard lesson of the earthquake: we all wanted to be saved by expertise, but we never were."[12]

Paul also told the young Harvard-trained professionals to beware of two pitfalls. First, he told them, *"the cause of the most costly failures are failures of imagination."* This happens when the very people who are charged with figuring out how to make things work instead become "socialized for scarcity" and fail to creatively imagine what is possible. Paul cautions against putting too much faith in metrics alone; the fact that there is no metric scale to measure creativity, virtue, or traits like "goodness or decency or social justice or patient accompaniment"[13] does not mean that virtuous traits and actions are not needed in public policy and in service for the common good. In fact, they are desperately needed, and their absence is often directly linked to failures.

The second warning Paul gave is to *"beware the iron cage of rationality."* He explains how bureaucracies, driven by the process of "routinization," have assumed power in modern society. While bureaucracy and routine have their benefits, such as improving efficiency, they have a terrible downside, as they decrease "the ability of human actors to be flexible, to respond to problems creatively and promptly." Paul argues that as organizations grow, they are likely to put emphasis on strengthening platforms of transparency and accountability. This overdependence on the "iron cage of rationality" gives top priority to organizational *systems,* and often the needs of *the people* being served are given a lesser priority. Innovation too is squashed in favor of adherence to following set rules and plans. There is little room in this system to apply the notion of accompaniment, which is "open-ended and egalitarian and elastic and nimble." Time and time again, Paul has seen the "the iron cage of rationality" lead to an "imaginative poverty, cynicism and disengagement,"[14] which inevitably hurt the poor.

Paul encouraged the graduates to partner with the poor, to link an option for the poor with accompaniment. He advised them to pay attention to matters like job creation to help lift people out of poverty, and to have an "open-source" view of the world that favors cooperation, openness, and teamwork. He urged them to consider adding a commitment to accompaniment to their skills and knowledge. It was an unusual speech; his topic and sources were not standard fare for Harvard-trained policy makers. Nevertheless, it was well received by students and faculty alike and, over the years, has been much quoted.

Sharing the Gift of Christian Hope

The spiritual practice of accompaniment is grounded in the "ministry of showing up." Accompaniment often involves, in the words of James Keenan, SJ, "being willing to enter into the chaos of another person's life."[15] Always personal and relational, even at the institutional level, accompaniment places emphasis on community building, receptive listening, presence, and open exchange. Accompaniment takes many forms, and it touches on all aspects of life—practical, spiritual, intellectual, financial, and moral. Accompaniment is a thoughtful process, where there is an awareness of the other person's feelings and needs. Accompaniment is often present in daily acts like listening with the heart, conversation, sharing in joys and sorrows, laughing and weeping, celebrating and mourning, sharing a meal, collaborating, waiting, visiting the sick, remembering important occasions, and helping to find needed goods and services. Being a good *accompagnateur* will always entail concrete actions and sacrifices, large and small, and frankly, it can sometimes be quite inconvenient. Paul has often been known to stop at the grocery and drugstore on the way to the airport to get just the kind of jelly a sick woman in Haiti asked for or nail clippers for an elderly gentleman whose grooming is important to him. We have lost count of how many Bibles and cell phones he has brought to people around the world. It took Paul three months to find the textbooks a young Rwandan man named Stephen asked for; Stephen is paralyzed from tuberculosis that invaded his spine but he had not given up on his dream of going to school. After finding the books, Paul found the funds for his tuition. The spiritual practice of accompaniment is filled with grace, mystery, and intimacy and involves "laying our lives down in little pieces, in small acts of sacrificial love and service. Part of the mystery is that while such concrete acts are costly, they nourish both the giver and the recipient."[16]

Paul believes in accompaniment because it "offers the surest means of protecting against the pitfalls inherent in our quests for personal efficacy and of moving forward, however slowly, toward equity, justice, compassion, and solidarity."[17] The words, actions, and attitudes embedded in the practice of accompaniment serve the reign of God preached by Jesus. Accompaniment is a hidden ground of love where "God's life rules, and in Jesus Christ, God heals divisions, reconciles the alienated, gives hope to those who have none, offers forgiveness to the sinner, includes the outcast."[18] Accompaniment makes God's healing love, mercy, and justice manifest, for "God's coming among us always passes through the face of another and through the banality of the humblest of gestures: dress, nourish, shelter, quench."[19] Faithfulness to the process of accompaniment, as Paul lives it out, is a vivid reminder that the calculus of the Gospel is not the calculus of the world, and that by focusing attention on the most vulnerable among us, it is *entirely possible* to show God's universal love to the poor. This is the fruit of the kind of accompaniment Paul practices on a daily basis, and it is how his actions bring about the building up of the kingdom of God on earth.

Bringing about the reign of God preached by Jesus leads to sharing the gift of Christian hope with our brothers and sisters. Paul knows that the Gospel of Jesus Christ demands that Christians turn their gaze towards the actual conditions that create hell on earth for their brothers and sisters. And this, in turn, means that Christians must share the gift of hope through concrete actions that will transform the lives of the suffering poor *in the here and now*. For Paul, this is a moral imperative. As Nathan Mitchell so aptly puts it, "For Christians, ethical practices like the preferential 'option' for the poor are not, in fact, optional. In a nutshell, no one gets into heaven without a letter of recommendation from the poor."[20] Paul recognizes that transforming the lives of the suffering poor is best accomplished through accompaniment, by walking with one's brothers and sisters on a path out of poverty into their full share of the life that God intends for humans—a life where God's reign in Jesus, through the power of the Spirit, is made present *in the here and now.*

A Request from Dr. Farmer and a Fitting Gift

I was with Paul in New York in March of 2018 when he gave a talk to a group of high-profile business executives. One of the things he told the crowd was how he was "coached to relate victory narratives." These victory narratives tell the story of projects and plans that have been successful. Paul surely has many wonderful victory narratives about extraordinary accomplishments over many years that are worthy of sharing with much gratitude, even with pride. Indeed, many such victory narratives have been shared in this book. Later that evening, after the event ended, Paul initiated a serious conversation with me. Since he had agreed to my writing this book a couple of years before, we had never discussed it again, so I was surprised when he brought it up. It was a short, intense conversation. In essence he said, "I only ask you to include one thing in the book. Please make sure you say that while I am grateful for the victory narratives, it is the unnecessary 'stupid deaths,' the terrible failures that we should not have let happen, that I think about most and that really upset me. Every person we lost that we should have saved is a terrible tragedy that I will never get over." Without comment, I have honored his request.

A few years ago, one of his former assistants, a wonderful young woman named Naomi Rosenberg, now an emergency room physician in Philadelphia, sent Paul a gift of two large posters, one of the corporal works of mercy, the other of the spiritual works of mercy. Designed by a graphic artist and printed on brown kraft paper with interesting black and red lettering, the posters are quite attractive and were, of course, a very thoughtful and meaningful gift. Paul loved the posters and immediately had them framed and hung over his bed. May the good doctor rest well under the words that inspire and guide his accompaniment of so many people the world over.

Abbreviated Time Line of Events in Paul Farmer's Life and Work

1959   Born on October 26 in North Adams, Massachusetts

1966   Moved to Birmingham, Alabama

1971   Moved to Brooksville, Florida

1982   Duke University, BA in Anthropology

1983   First trip to Haiti

1984   • Death of Paul Farmer Sr. on July 22

       • Entered Harvard Medical School

1987   • Founding of Partners In Health with Ophelia Dahl, Jim Kim, Todd McCormack, and Tom White

       • Zanmi Lasante, first PIH sister organization, officially founded in Haiti

1990   • Harvard Medical School, MD

       • Harvard University, PhD in Anthropology

1992   • *AIDS and Accusation: Haiti and the Geography of Blame*

       • Socios en Salud, second PIH sister organization, founded in Peru

1994   *The Uses of Haiti*

1995   Death of Fr. Jack Roussin on June 9

1996
- Marriage to Didi Bertrand
- *Women, Poverty and AIDS: Sex, Drugs and Structural Violence*
- PIH and Socios en Salud begin treating MDRTB patients in Peru

1998
- Birth of Catherine Bertrand Farmer on January 13
- PIH establishes Партнеры во имя здоровья, a sister organization in Russia

1999
Infections and Inequalities: The Modern Plagues

2003
- *Mountains Beyond Mountains: The Quest of Dr. Paul Farmer, a Man Who Would Cure the World*, by Tracy Kidder
- *Pathologies of Power: Health, Human Rights, and the New War on Poverty*

2004
Getting Haiti Right This Time: The U.S. and the Coup, edited by Noam Chomsky, Paul Farmer, and Amy Goodman

2005
PIH establishes Inshuti Mu Buzima, a sister organization in Rwanda

2006
PIH establishes Bo-Mphato Litšebeletsong tsa Bophelo, a sister organization in Lesotho

2007
- Birth of Elisabeth Grace Farmer on September 21
- PIH establishes Abwenzi Pa Za Umoyo, a sister organization in Malawi

2008
Birth of Charles Sebastien Farmer on February 22

2009
- PIH establishes sister organization in the Navajo Nation
- Named chair of the Department of Global Health and Social Medicine at HMS
- Named United Nations Deputy Special Envoy to Haiti under former president Bill Clinton
- *Global Health in Times of Violence*, edited by Barbara Rylko-Bauer, Linda Whiteford, and Paul Farmer

2010 • Earthquake in Haiti on January 12

• Named Kolokotrones University Professor at Harvard University

• *Partner to the Poor: A Paul Farmer Reader,* edited by Haun Saussy

2011 • Death of Tom White on January 9

• *Haiti after the Earthquake*

• PIH establishes Compañeros en Salud, a sister organization in Mexico

2012 Named special adviser to the United Nations secretary-general

2013 • *In the Company of the Poor: Conversations with Dr. Paul Farmer and Fr. Gustavo Gutiérrez,* edited by Michael Griffin and Jennie Weiss Block

• *To Repair the World: Paul Farmer Speaks to the Next Generation,* edited by Jonathan Weigel

• *Reimagining Global Health: An Introduction,* edited by Paul Farmer, Jim Yon Kim, Arthur Kleinman, and Matthew Basilico

• Opening of Hôpital Universitaire de Mirebalais, Mirebalais, Haiti

2014 PIH begins work in Liberia and Sierra Leone during the Ebola epidemic

Notes

Introduction—pages 1–12

1. Tracy Kidder, *Mountains Beyond Mountains: The Quest of Dr. Paul Farmer, a Man Who Would Cure the World* (New York: Random House, 2003), 294.

2. Mark Klempner, "A Conversation with Tracy Kidder about *Mountains Beyond Mountains*," *Huffington Post*, May 25, 2011, https://www.huffingtonpost.com/mark-klempner/a-conversation-with-tracy_b_91799.html.

3. Paul Farmer and Gustavo Gutiérrez, *In the Company of the Poor: Conversations with Dr. Paul Farmer and Fr. Gustavo Gutiérrez*, ed. Michael Griffin and Jennie Weiss Block (Maryknoll, NY: Orbis Books, 2013), 31.

4. An abbreviated time line of Paul's life and work, including many events not covered in this book, is provided at the end of the book.

Chapter One: A Bus, a Boat, and Some Big Ideas—pages 13–28

1. Paul Farmer, "Q and A: Health Care for the Poorest as a Central Human Right," interview by Patricia Cohen, *New York Times*, March 29, 2003.

2. Paul Farmer and Gustavo Gutiérrez, *In the Company of the Poor: Conversations with Dr. Paul Farmer and Fr. Gustavo Gutiérrez*, ed. Michael Griffin and Jennie Weiss Block (Maryknoll, NY: Orbis Books, 2013), 15.

3. Farmer, "Q&A."

4. Tracy Kidder, *Mountains Beyond Mountains: The Quest of Dr. Paul Farmer, a Man Who Would Cure the World* (New York: Random House, 2003), 50.

5. Jennifer Farmer, e-mail message to author, June 19, 2017.

6. Ibid.

7. Dan DeWitt, "In Haiti, Paul Farmer's Charity Partners In Health Makes a Difference," *Tampa Bay Times*, December 13, 2008.

8. "On the Evolution of an Applied Anthropologist and Healer: An Interview with Paul Farmer," by Barbara Rylko-Bauer, Society for Applied Anthropology, April 2, 2016, http://sfaa.net/news/index.php/2017/may-2017/oral-history/evolution-applied-anthropologist-and-healer-interview-paul-farmer/.

9. Ibid.

10. Farmer and Gutiérrez, *Company*, 16.

11. Kidder, *Mountains*, 62.

12. Ibid.

13. Melinda Gates, commencement address, Duke University, May 12, 2013, www.gatesfoundation.org/Media-Center/Speeches/2013/05/Melinda-Gates-Duke-Commencement-2013.

14. Rylko-Bauer, "On the Evolution."

15. Ibid.

16. Paul Farmer, *To Repair the World: Paul Farmer Speaks to the Next Generation*, ed. Jonathan L. Weigel (Los Angeles: University of California Press, 2013), 21.

Chapter Two: The Corporal Works of Mercy: Weapons of Mass Salvation—pages 29–47

1. Paul Farmer, *To Repair the World: Paul Farmer Speaks to the Next Generation*, ed. Jonathan L. Weigel (Los Angeles: University of California Press, 2013), 187.

2. Ibid., 137.

3. Fr. Gerry died in 2009 from the complications of a stroke. Paul remained actively involved in his life and his treatment until the end. He shared his sentiments about Fr. Gerry with John Dear in an article John wrote in the *National Catholic Reporter*: "Fr. Gerry Jean-Juste was a lot more than a hero and a friend. He was more than a defender

of Haitian refugees. Fr. Gerry was more than a prisoner of conscience, just as he was more than a tireless advocate for the poor and marginalized, wherever they live (and, too often, die untimely). Gerry was more than a noted human rights campaigner, and more, even, than a voice for the voiceless, a prophet. Gerry was also, and (to me, most importantly) a humble parish priest who worried about such mundane matters as feeding the hungry, clothing the naked, and visiting the prisoners. Even when he was himself imprisoned unjustly, he took these and other charges seriously. We will miss Fr. Gerry more than we can say and must do all we can to continue his efforts to promote the dignity of all of God's children." John Dear, "My Rosary Is My Only Weapon," *National Catholic Reporter*, June 16, 2009, https://www.ncronline.org/blogs/road-peace/my-rosary-my-only-weapon.

4. Ophelia Dahl, commencement address, Wellesley College, May 2006, https://www.wellesley.edu/events/commencement/archives/2006commencement/commencementaddress.

5. "On the Evolution of an Applied Anthropologist and Healer: An Interview with Paul Farmer," by Barbara Rylko-Bauer, Society for Applied Anthropology, April 2, 2016,

6. This event is told in greater detail in Kidder, *Mountains*, 80–81.

7. Ibid., 81.

8. Paul Farmer, " Listening for Prophetic Voices in Medicine," *America* 177 (July 1997): 8.

9. Ibid., 9.

10. Paul Farmer and Gustavo Gutiérrez, *In the Company of the Poor: Conversations with Dr. Paul Farmer and Fr. Gustavo Gutiérrez*, ed. Michael Griffin and Jennie Weiss Block (Maryknoll, NY: Orbis Books, 2013), 20. This insight was first developed in the social sciences; liberation theologians found it applicable to their theological project and incorporated it into their work.

11. Kidder, *Mountains*, 84.

12. Ibid., 79.

13. The Partners In Health mission statement, which has remained the same since its founding, is as follows: "To provide a preferential option for the poor in health care. By establishing long-term relationships with sister organizations based in settings of poverty, Partners In Health strives to achieve two overarching goals: to bring the benefits of modern medical science to those most in need of them and to

serve as an antidote to despair. We draw on the resources of the world's leading academic medical and academic institutions and the lived experience of the world's poorest and sickest communities. At its root, our mission is both medical and moral. It is based on solidarity rather than charity alone. When our patients are ill and have no access to health care, our team of health professionals, scholars and activists will do whatever it takes to make them well—just as we would do for a member of our own family." 2015 *Annual Report for Partners In Health*, https://www.pih.org/pages/2015-annual-report.

14. Farmer and Gutiérrez, *Company*, 31.

Chapter Three: Coupling Inquiry and Implementation: Making a Preferential Option for the Poor in Health Care—pages 48–72

1. Paul Farmer, *To Repair the World: Paul Farmer Speaks to the Next Generation*, ed. Jonathan L. Weigel (Los Angeles: University of California Press, 2013), 17.

2. Ibid., 203.

3. Ibid., 58.

4. Paul Farmer and Gustavo Gutiérrez, *In the Company of the Poor: Conversations with Dr. Paul Farmer and Fr. Gustavo Gutiérrez*, ed. Michael Griffin and Jennie Weiss Block (Maryknoll, NY: Orbis Books, 2013), 16.

5. Ibid., 20.

6. For an in-depth discussion of Dr. Farmer's use of liberation theology in his medical work, see chapter 5 of Paul Farmer, *Pathologies of Power: Health, Human Rights, and the New War on the Poor* (Berkeley: University of California Press, 2003).

7. *In the Company of the Poor: Conversations with Dr. Paul Farmer and Fr. Gustavo Gutiérrez* is the fruit of this conference and contains, among other things, the talks presented at Notre Dame by both men and an in-depth interview with them.

8. Farmer and Gutiérrez, *Company*, 19–22.

9. Ibid., 24.

10. Fr. Gustavo's talk was entitled "Saying and Showing to the Poor: 'God Loves You.'" Ibid., 27–34.

11. Paul Farmer, "The Power of the Poor in Haiti," *America* 164 (March 1991): 260.

12. Paul Farmer, Jim Yong Kim, Arthur Kleinman, and Matthew Basilico, eds., *Reimagining Global Health: An Introduction* (Berkeley: University of California Press, 2013), 9.

13. Ibid., 2.

14. Quoted in Paul Farmer, *AIDS and Accusation: Haiti and the Geography of Blame* (Berkeley: University of California Press, 1992), 252.

15. Farmer, "The Power of the Poor," 264.

16. Ibid., 260.

17. Cecilia González-Andrieu, "A Life Lived in God's Love," *America* 215 (March 6, 2017): 20.

18. This event is told in some detail in Dr. Farmer's 2005 Tanner Lecture, "Never Again? Reflections on Human Values and Human Rights," and is included in Haun Saussy, ed., *Partner to the Poor: A Paul Farmer Reader* (Berkeley: University of California Press, 2010), 507–8.

19. Aristide had left the priesthood in 1994 and in 1998 was expelled from the Salesians, after years of tension about his political views and career, and his open critique of the church hierarchy. Like the liberation theology he espouses, Aristide has many detractors, and he remains a controversial figure, as revolutionaries and radicals often are. Several years after leaving the priesthood, Aristide married a Haitian American lawyer, Mildred Trouillot, with whom he had two daughters. Mildred and "Titid," as he is affectionately called by his close friends, returned to Haiti in March of 2011, after living in exile in South Africa for seven years. Aristide is out of the public square these days and dedicates his time to building social and educational programs in Haiti. Paul sits on the board of one of Aristide's projects, UNIFA, a medical school whose mission is to provide medical training to talented young people from poor families. Aristide is still beloved by many of the Haitian poor, and "TITID" is scrawled on walls throughout Haiti. Just recently, there was yet another assassination attempt on his life, perhaps the fourth or fifth. Paul remains close to Aristide and his family and sometimes stops by for a visit with his old friend.

20. Paul Farmer, *The Uses of Haiti* (Monroe, ME: Common Courage Press, 1994), 13.

21. Ibid., 6.

22. Ibid.

23. Howard Hiatt, "Learn from Haiti," December 6, 2001, https://www.nytimes.com/2001/12/06/opinion/learn-from-haiti.html.

24. Ibid.

25. Paul Farmer, *Infections and Inequalities: The Modern Plagues* (Berkeley: University of California Press, 1999), 30.

26. Ibid.

27. Ibid., 31.

28. Tracy Kidder, *Mountains Beyond Mountains: The Quest of Dr. Paul Farmer, a Man Who Would Cure the World* (New York: Random House, 2003), 126.

29. World Health Organization, "Tuberculosis (TB)," http://www.who.int/tb/en/.

30. Farmer, *Infections and Inequalities*, 33.

31. Ibid.

32. Farmer, *To Repair*, 16.

33. Farmer, *Infections and Inequalities*, 33.

34. Kidder, *Mountains*, 182.

35. Ibid.

36. "New Guidelines and Goals for Treating MDR-TB Announced," Partners In Health website, June 5, 2006, https://pih.org/article/new-guidelines-and-goals-for-treating-mdr-tb-announced.

Chapter Four: Mountains, Pathologies, No Cheap Grace: Towards Global Health Equity—pages 73–96

1. Paul Farmer, *To Repair the World: Paul Farmer Speaks to the Next Generation*, ed. Jonathan L. Weigel (Los Angeles: University of California Press, 2013), 5.

2. Paul Farmer, *Pathologies of Power: Health, Human Rights, and the New War on the Poor* (Berkeley: University of California Press, 2003), 20.

3. Ibid., 255.

4. Steven Miles, review of *Pathologies of Power: Health, Human Rights, and the New War on the Poor* by Paul Farmer, *New England*

Journal of Medicine 350, no. 7 (2004), 737, https://www.nejm.org/doi/full/10.1056/NEJM200402123500724.

5. Herbert Abrams, review of *Pathologies of Power: Health, Human Rights, and the New War on the Poor,* by Paul Farmer, *Journal of Public Health Policy* 25, no. 2 (2004): 234, http://www.jstor.org/stable/3343427.

6. Farmer, *Pathologies of Power,* 255–56.

7. Thomas Merton, *The Seven Storey Mountain* (New York: Harcourt, Brace and Company, 1948), 422.

8. This speech is published in *To Repair the World: Paul Farmer Speaks to the Next Generation.* Edited by one of Paul's former students, Jon Weigel, with a foreword by President Bill Clinton, the book is a compilation of nineteen of Paul's speeches. It is an accessible book that, in the words of Dr. Jim Kim, "brings us close to Paul Farmer in a way that scholarly publications can't." The book reveals different sides of Paul: his gentleness, his wit, his passion for justice, his love of the poor, and his ability to connect with young people.

9. Farmer, *To Repair,* 28.

10. Ibid.

11. The Clinton Health Access Initiative, Inc. (CHAI), was founded in 2002. Its ambitious goal was to help save the lives of millions of people living with HIV/AIDS in the developing world, and its dedicated efforts have been extremely successful.

12. Paul Farmer, *Haiti after the Earthquake,* ed. Abbey Gardner and Cassia Van Der Hoof Holstein (New York: Public Affairs, 2011), 223.

13. Dr. Agnes Binagwaho and others, "Rwanda 20 Years On: Investing in Life," *The Lancet* 384 (July 2014): 371.

14. Farmer, *Haiti after the Earthquake,* 224.

15. Ibid., 219.

16. "The World Bank in Rwanda," November 6, 2017, www.worldbank.org/en/country/rwanda/overview.

17. Bella English, "In Rwanda, Visionary Doctor Is Moving Mountains Again," *Boston Globe,* April 13, 2008.

18. Ophelia Dahl, "Ophelia Dahl Reports from PIH-Supported Hospital in Rwinkwavu, Rwanda," Partners In Health website, June 24, 2011, https://pih.org/article/ophelia-dahl-reports-from-pih-supported-hospital-in-rwinkwavu-rwanda.

19. Paul Farmer, "Rwanda Rebuilt," in MASS Design Group, *Empowering Architecture: The Butaro Hospital, Rwanda* (Boston: MASS Design Group, 2011), 22.

20. Ibid.

21. Michael Igoe, "Paul Farmer's 'Lifelong Dream,'" *Devex*, September 17, 2015, devex.com/news/paul-farmer-s-lifelong dream-86915.

22. Ibid.

23. The only other universities in the world offering this degree are Harvard and Dartmouth.

24. Wonkborg, "Paul Farmer's Graph of the Year: Rwanda's Plummeting Child Mortality Rate," *Wonkblog, Washington Post*, December 29, 2013, https://www.washingtonpost.com/news/wonk/wp/2013/12/29/paul-farmers-graph-of-the-year-rwandas-plummeting-child-mortality-rate/?utm_term=.aeabee22929b.

25. Howard Hiatt, MD, is founder and associate chief of the Division of Global Health Equity at the Brigham. Dr. Hiatt has been a transformative force in global health equity, and he and his late wife, Doris, have enriched the lives of thousands of students, including Paul since his student days. Dr. Hiatt is also one of the kindest and most generous men on the planet.

26. Farmer, *Pathologies of Power*, 146.

Chapter Five: Fighting the Long Defeat: Making Common Cause with the Losers—pages 97–127

1. Tracy Kidder, *Mountains Beyond Mountains: The Quest of Dr. Paul Farmer, a Man Who Would Cure the World* (New York: Random House, 2003), 288.

2. "Haiti: UN Envoy Bill Clinton Appoints Prominent US Doctor as Deputy," *UN News*, August 11, 2009, https://news.un.org/en/story/2009/08/309352-haiti-un-envoy-bill-clinton-appoints-prominent-us-doctor-deputy.

3. United Press International, "Bill Clinton Tapped as U.N. Envoy to Haiti," May 19, 2009, https://www.upi.com/Bill-Clinton-tapped-as-UN-envoy-to-Haiti/92751242766947/print.

4. Trenton Daniel, "UN's Deputy Special Envoy to Haiti Wraps Up First Trip," *Miami Herald*, September 9, 2010.

5. Paul Farmer, *Haiti after the Earthquake*, ed. Abbey Gardner and Cassia Van Der Hoof Holstein (New York: Public Affairs, 2011), 39.

6. Ibid., 39

7. Ibid., 40.

8. Ibid., 41.

9. Ibid., 42.

10. Ibid.

11. Bellerive replaced Pierre-Louis as prime minister in November when, in an unfortunate turn of events, Pierre-Louis was ousted by the senate.

12. Farmer, *Haiti after the Earthquake*, 58.

13. Ibid., 60.

14. Ibid.

15. Ibid., 61.

16. Ibid., 62.

17. Ibid., 63.

18. Ibid., 20.

19. Ibid., 61.

20. Kathleen M. O'Connor, *Lamentations and the Tears of the World* (Maryknoll, NY: Orbis Books, 2002), 78.

21. Testimony of Dr. Paul Farmer to the US Senate Committee on Foreign Relations, January 27, 2010, https://www.foreign.senate.gov/imo/media/doc/FarmerTestimony100128a.pdf.

22. O'Connor, *Lamentations*, 102.

23. Farmer, *Haiti after the Earthquake*, 69.

24. Ibid., 75.

25. Ibid., 76.

26. Ibid., 77.

27. Ibid., 87.

28. Ibid., 210.

29. Ibid., 199.

30. Ibid., 188–89.

31. These estimates are likely low, as many cases in rural areas went unreported.

32. Led by Dr. Louis Ivers, the effort vaccinated 45,417 patients, each receiving two doses of the drug two weeks apart. The results were excellent, with about 65 percent fewer cholera cases among

people who had been vaccinated than in those who were unvaccinated. As a result of the PIH vaccination campaign, the Haitian Ministry of Health, with the support of their partners, administered the vaccine to 300,000 citizens, and the World Health Organization has begun stockpiling the drug for use in future outbreaks. "Cholera Vaccine Succeeds in Haiti," February 20, 2015, https://www.pih.org /article/cholera-vaccine-succeeds-in-haiti-louise-ivers-lancet.

33. Farmer, *Haiti after the Earthquake*, 161.

34. Paul Farmer, speech, Croix-des-Bouquets, Haiti, December 21, 2014, tape recording.

Chapter Six: Who Lives? Who Dies?: Access to Health Care as a Human Right—pages 128–48

1. Paul Farmer, "Who Lives and Who Dies: Paul Farmer on the Iniquities of Healthcare Funding," *London Review of Books* 37, no. 3 (February 2015): 17–20.

2. Paul Farmer, *Haiti after the Earthquake*, ed. Abbey Gardner and Cassia Van Der Hoof Holstein (New York: Public Affairs, 2011), 162–63.

3. Ibid., 239.

4. Ibid., 237.

5. Ibid., 243.

6. The estimates of the numbers who died during or because of the earthquake are between 250,000 and 325,000.

7. Farmer, *Haiti after the Earthquake*, 241.

8. Along with significant private philanthropy from many generous individuals, the following is a partial list of the organizations and corporations that contributed to help build and support the Mirebalais hospital: American Red Cross, Artists for Haiti, Covidien, Entertainment Industry Foundation, GE Foundation, Hewlett-Packard, MacArthur Foundation, and W. K. Kellogg Foundation.

9. For a longer discussion on the work of the Interim Haiti Recovery Commission, see pages 156–58, 211–12, 248–49 of *Haiti after the Earthquake*.

10. Jake Johnston, "Where Does the Money Go? Eight Years of USAID Funding in Haiti," Center for Economic and Policy Research,

January 11, 2018, http://cepr.net/blogs/haiti-relief-and-reconstruction-watch/where-does-the-money-go-eight-years-of-usaid-funding-in-haiti.

11. Centers for Disease Control and Prevention, "2014–2016 Ebola Outbreak in West Africa," December 27, 2017, https://www.cdc.gov/vhf/ebola/outbreaks/2014-west-africa/index.html. The 28,652 figure includes "reported, suspected or probable" cases. Both the number of cases and the death count are likely to be higher, as many people were unable to seek treatment and died at home.

12. Paul Farmer, "The Caregivers' Disease," *London Review of Books* 37, no. 10 (May 2015): 25–28.

13. Felice Freyer, "Partners In Health Staff to Join African Ebola Fight," *Boston Globe*, September 15, 2014.

14. Paul Farmer, "The Secret to Curing West Africa from Ebola Is No Secret at All," *Washington Post*, January 16, 2015, https://www.washingtonpost.com/opinions/paul-farmer-the-secret-to-curing-west-africa-from-ebola-is-no-secret-at-all/2015/01/16/658a6686-9cb9-11e4-bcfb-059ec7a93ddc_story.html?utm_term=.85b565a014ca.

15. Paul Farmer and Rajesh Panjabi, "Ebola Does Not Need to Be a Death Sentence," *Huffington Post*, October 16, 2014, http://www.huffingtonpost.com/paulfarmer/ebola-does-not-need-to-be_b_5996652.html.

16. Andrew S. Boozary, Paul Farmer, and Ashish K. Jha, "The Ebola Outbreak, Fragile Health Systems and Quality as a Cure," *Journal of the American Medical Association* 312, no. 18 (November 2014): 1859–60.

17. Paul Farmer, "Who Lives and Who Dies," 17–20.

18. Boozary, Farmer, and Jha, "The Ebola Outbreak."

19. Ibid.

20. Ibid.

21. Ibid.

22. See Boozary, Farmer, and Jha, "The Ebola Outbreak," for a discussion on the cost analysis of providing safe and effective care.

23. Paul has poured his heart and soul into *Fevers, Feuds and Diamonds*, which is being published by Farrar, Straus and Giroux and scheduled to be released in 2019. Don't miss reading it!

Conclusion: Accompaniment: Sharing the Gift of Christian Hope—pages 149–59

1. Paul Farmer, *To Repair the World: Paul Farmer Speaks to the Next Generation*, ed. Jonathan L. Weigel (Los Angeles: University of California Press, 2013), 246.

2. Paul Farmer and Gustavo Gutiérrez, *In the Company of the Poor: Conversations with Dr. Paul Farmer and Fr. Gustavo Gutiérrez*, ed. Michael Griffin and Jennie Weiss Block (Maryknoll, NY: Orbis Books, 2013), 27.

3. Farmer, *To Repair*, 235.

4. Jean Vanier, *Becoming Human* (Toronto, ON: Anashi Press, 1998), 129–30.

5. Roberto S. Goizueta, *Caminemos con Jesús: Towards a Hispanic/Latino Theology of Accompaniment* (Maryknoll, NY: Orbis Books, 1995), 209.

6. Ibid.

7. Farmer, *To Repair*, 234.

8. Ibid., 236.

9. Joia Mukherjee and Eddy Eustache, "Community Health Workers as a Cornerstone for Integrating HIV and Primary Healthcare," *AIDS Care* 19, Supplement I (2007): 80.

10. Farmer, *To Repair*, 245.

11. Ibid., 244.

12. Ibid.

13. Ibid., 245.

14. Ibid.

15. James F. Keenan, *The Works of Mercy: The Heart of Catholicism* (Lanham, MD: Rowman & Littlefield, 2005), 3.

16. Christine D. Pohl, *Making Room: Recovering Hospitality as a Christian Tradition* (Grand Rapids, MI: W. B. Eerdmans, 1999), 71.

17. Farmer and Gutiérrez, *Company*, 181.

18. Catherine Mowry LaCugna, *God for Us: The Trinity and Christian Life* (San Francisco: Harper Collins, 1991), 335.

19. Nathan D. Mitchell, *Meeting Mystery: Liturgy, Worship, Sacraments* (Maryknoll, NY: Orbis Books, 2006), 42.

20. Ibid., 41.

Selected Bibliography

Primary Sources

Boozary, Andrew S., Paul Farmer, and Ashish K. Jha. "The Ebola Outbreak, Fragile Health Systems and Quality as a Cure." *Journal of the American Medical Association* 312, no. 18 (November 2014): 1859–60.

Chomsky, Noam, Paul Farmer, and Amy Goodman, eds. *Getting Haiti Right This Time: The U.S. and the Coup.* Monroe, ME: Common Courage Press, 2004.

Farmer, Paul. *AIDS and Accusation: Haiti and the Geography of Blame.* Berkeley: University of California Press, 1992.

———. "The Caregivers' Disease." *London Review of Books* 37, no. 10 (May 2015): 25–28.

———. *Haiti after the Earthquake.* Edited by Abbey Gardner and Cassia Van Der Hoof Holstein. New York: Public Affairs, 2011.

———. *Infections and Inequalities: The Modern Plagues.* Berkeley: University of California Press, 1999.

———. "Listening for Prophetic Voices in Medicine." *America* 177 (July 1997): 8.

———. "On the Evolution of an Applied Anthropologist and Healer: An Interview with Paul Farmer." By Barbara Rylko-Bauer. Society for Applied Anthropology, April 2, 2016.

———. *Pathologies of Power: Health, Human Rights, and the New War on the Poor.* Berkeley: University of California Press, 2003.

———. "The Power of the Poor in Haiti." *America* 164 (March 1991): 260.

———. "Rwanda Rebuilt." In *Empowering Architecture: The Butaro Hospital, Rwanda,* edited by Michael Murphy and Alan Ricks, 22–27. Boston: MASS Design Group, 2011.

———. "The Secret to Curing West Africa from Ebola is No Secret at All." *Washington Post,* January 16, 2015.

———. *To Repair the World: Paul Farmer Speaks to the Next Generation.* Edited by Jonathan L. Weigel. Los Angeles: University of California Press, 2013.

———. *The Uses of Haiti.* Monroe, ME: Common Courage Press, 1994.

———. "Who Lives and Who Dies: Paul Farmer on the Iniquities of Healthcare Funding." *London Review of Books* 37, no. 3 (February 2015): 17–20.

Farmer, Paul, and Gustavo Gutiérrez. *In the Company of the Poor: Conversations with Dr. Paul Farmer and Fr. Gustavo Gutiérrez.* Edited by Michael Griffin and Jennie Weiss Block. Maryknoll, NY: Orbis Books, 2013.

Farmer, Paul, Jim Yong Kim, Arthur Kleinman, and Matthew Basilico, eds. *Reimagining Global Health: An Introduction.* Berkeley: University of California Press, 2013.

Farmer, Paul, Margaret Connors, and Janie Simmons, eds. *Women, Poverty, and AIDS: Sex, Drugs, and Structural Violence.* Monroe, ME: Common Courage Press, 1996.

Farmer, Paul and Rajesh Panjabi. "Ebola Does Not Need to Be a Death Sentence." *Huffington Post,* October 16, 2014.

Kidder, Tracy. *Mountains Beyond Mountains: The Quest of Dr. Paul Farmer, a Man Who Would Cure the World.* New York: Random House, 2003.

Rylko-Bauer, Barbara, Linda Whiteford, and Paul Farmer, eds. *Global Health in Times of Violence.* Santa Fe, NM: SAR Press, 2009.

Saussy, Haun, ed. *Partner to the Poor: A Paul Farmer Reader.* Berkeley: University of California Press, 2010.

Secondary Sources

Abrams, Herbert. Review of *Pathologies of Power: Health, Human Rights, and the New War on the Poor*, by Paul Farmer. *Journal of Public Health Policy* 25, no. 2 (2004): 234.

Binagwaho, Agnes, and others. "Rwanda 20 Years On: Investing in Life." *The Lancet* 384 (July 2014): 371.

Dahl, Ophelia. "Commencement Address." Wellesley College, May 2006.

DeWitt, Dan. "In Haiti, Paul Farmer's Charity Partners In Health Makes a Difference." *Tampa Bay Times*, December 13, 2008.

English, Bella. "In Rwanda, Visionary Doctor Is Moving Mountains Again." *Boston Globe*, April 13, 2008.

Farmer, Paul. "Q and A: Health Care for the Poorest as a Central Human Right." Interview by Patricia Cohen. *New York Times*, March 29, 2003.

Freyer, Felice. "Partners In Health Staff to Join African Ebola Fight." *Boston Globe*, September 15, 2014.

Gates, Melinda. "Commencement Address." Duke University, May 12, 2013.

Goizueta, Roberto S. *Caminemos con Jesús: Towards a Hispanic/ Latino Theology of Accompaniment*. Maryknoll, NY: Orbis Books, 1995.

González-Andrieu, Cecilia. "A Life Lived in God's Love." *America* 215 (March 2017): 20.

Igoe, Michael. "Paul Farmer's 'Lifelong Dream.'" *Devex*, September 17, 2015. Devex.com/news/paul-farmer-s-lifelong dream-86915.

Johnston, Jake. "Where Does the Money Go? Eight Years of USAID Funding in Haiti." Blog of the Center for Economic and Policy Research, January 11, 2018. http://cepr.net/blogs/haiti-relief-and-reconstruction-watch/where-does-the-money-go-eight-years-of-usaid-funding-in-haiti.

Keenan, James F. *The Works of Mercy: The Heart of Catholicism*. Lanham, MD: Rowman & Littlefield Publications, 2005.

LaCugna, Catherine Mowry. *God for Us: The Trinity and Christian Life*. San Francisco: Harper Collins, 1991.

Merton, Thomas. *The Seven Storey Mountain*. New York: Harcourt, Brace and Company, 1948.

Miles, Steven. Review of *Pathologies of Power: Health, Human Rights, and the New War on the Poor*, by Paul Farmer. *New England Journal of Medicine* 350, no. 7 (2004): 737.

Mitchell, Nathan D. *Meeting Mystery: Liturgy, Worship, Sacraments*. Maryknoll, NY: Orbis Books, 2006.

Mukherjee, Joia, and Eddy Eustache. "Community Health Workers as a Cornerstone for Integrating HIV and Primary Healthcare." *AIDS Care* 19, Supplement I (2007): 80.

O'Connor, Kathleen M. *Lamentations and the Tears of the World*. Maryknoll, NY: Orbis Books, 2002.

Pohl, Christine D. *Making Room: Recovering Hospitality as a Christian Tradition*. Grand Rapids, MI: W. B. Eerdmans, 1999.

Vanier, Jean. *Becoming Human*. Toronto: Anashi Press, 1998.

Wonkborg. "Paul Farmer's Graph of the Year: Rwanda's Plummeting Child Mortality Rate." *Wonkblog, Washington Post*, December 29, 2013.

Index